P9-BZV-872

347
WOODWORKING PATTERNS

**A Bound Set of Popular
Woodworking Patterns**

Acknowledgements

For their creative contributions, thanks to Jeanne Uecker, Ginger Fulton, Dale Crum and David Dixon.

Special thanks to Patti Lynn, Diane Dunn, Natalie Cawood, and Monika Orleck for their diligent work and long hours in compiling this book. Thank you Linda, for your excellent proofing skills. Thanks to Diane K. for her writing skills.

Above all, we acknowledge Jesus Christ, who gives us life, love and happiness and shows us true beauty.

In all thy ways acknowledge him, and he shall direct thy paths.

Proverbs 3:6

All rights reserved. Printed in the United States of America. This book may not be reproduced or distributed in any form or by any means without permission of the publisher. For information or to order copies contact:

©1990, 1991, 1992   FC&A
103 Clover Green
Peachtree City, GA 30269

Fifteenth edition printed April 1992

We have made every effort to ensure the accuracy and completeness of these patterns and drawings. We cannot, however, be responsible for human error, typographical mistakes, or variations in individual work.

ISBN # 0-915099-26-8

Cover Design by Debbie Williams & Diane Dunn

Table of Contents

Metric Conversion Chart

Measurements: simply apply metric units to most of the pattern grids instead of the inches and feet suggested in the text.

In the U.S.A., lumber generally is measured in inches, such as 2 inches by 4 inches, 1 inch by 2 inches, etc. For example, what you know as a 100x50mm (4 inches by 2 inches) stud would be called a 2x4 throughout the pattern book. A 2440x1220mm sheet of plywood would be a 4x8-foot sheet in this book.

Most building and decorating materials in the UK are sold in metric units, but you may find both metric and Imperial units like inches and feet being used side-by-side in some retail establishments. Here is a table you may use to convert from Imperial to metric units:

To convert	Into	Multiply by
inches	millimetres	25.4
feet	metres	0.305
yards	metres	0.914
millimetres	inches	0.394
metres	feet	3.28
metres	yards	1.094

INTRODUCTION

For every craft there is a pattern. But just trying to find the patterns that you want, when you want them is one of the most frustrating problems that faces the hobbiest today. If you can't make a mental picture and create the pattern from it, you pretty much have to settle for what's on the market, and the choices aren't always great.

If you've been woodworking for quite a while or are very artistic and creative, designing your own patterns is probably very easy for you. However, for most of us, it's almost impossible. Even if the artistic talent is there, coming up with new ideas that really work isn't easy.

The coming decade should offer many creative opportunities for the home hobbiest. Woodworkers everywhere are finding that it requires a major investment of time and money to build a good library of patterns. Even when you can find a pattern that you like, chances are that you will have to change its dimensions, size it up or try to decipher the directions. New and imaginative ideas always seem to belong to someone else.

Get ready for a surprise!

A new world of woodworking is about to unfold with the publication of the book, "347 Woodworking Patterns." This book is filled with page after page of patterns to suit any decor and all tastes. Make those special projects that you have dreamed that you could create.

You will find beginner patterns as well as more complex patterns for the woodworker looking for a challenge. The selection of patterns will astonish you.

Some are "tried and true" — patterns that have been around, but no matter how often you see them, you still want to make them just one more time. Others are fantastic new ideas that you've never seen before seeing this book!

Once you take a look at this book, you won't be able to wait to get started on a project.

But have a little patience.

Look at all the information contained in this book. As well as hundreds of patterns, we give you tips on painting, finishing, easy-to-understand instructions and so much more. Once you've used this book, you will never be satisfied with regular run-of-the-mill projects again. The rewards of satisfaction and pride in a project well-done are yours just by using this book.

Before beginning any project, there are some things that should be considered.

FOR YOUR SAFETY

Always make sure you are well protected. Be sure to follow all the directions and safety procedures included in the owner's manual that came with your saw. Those instructions can save you time and money.

Safety glasses or goggles should always be worn. Remember, you only have one pair of eyes; dust motes and splinters hurt!

Make sure that all clothing on the upper body fits tightly. Loose-fitting clothing can be easily pulled into machinery.

Secure all machinery to a workbench or stand. Vibrations can cause saws to shift and fall off. Be sure to turn off all machinery when you are not using it.

Never leave electrical cords in the work area to eliminate the extra hazard of tripping over them.

When feeding wood into the saw blade, use both hands and keep a steady pressure. Forcing the wood can cause the blade to break or can push the wood off course.

Pushing wood into the side of the blade or trying to turn a radius too small for the blade can also break the blade or push it off course. Breaking blades is not only hazardous, but is also expensive.

CHOOSING YOUR TOOLS

The tools that you use will help determine the way your finished project looks. Naturally, high-quality tools will perform better and last longer than lower-quality tools. Remember to keep all tools oiled and clean. Build-up of dust and grime impair machine function.

The most important tool in your workshop is your saw. There are three basic types of saws: a scroll saw, a band saw and a jig saw. All three can be used to cut the patterns in the book. The scroll saw is probably the easiest to work with, but always work with the one that is the most comfortable for you.

Make sure you keep plenty of extra saw blades on hand. When cutting intricate designs, especially on a scroll saw, the blade could break if too much pressure is applied. So, always keep a spare or two, just in case.

It's a fact: the sharper the blade, the finer the cut. To cut down on sanding time, always keep blades sharp.

Keep a hammer, ruler, sandpaper or sanding block handy. A drill with an assortment of bits and a set of screwdrivers are absolute necessities.

A router is always a nice touch, and will certainly give your projects a nice finishing touch. Try to keep some organization in your workshop. Constantly hunting for a tool can cause undue stress and take the enjoyment out of a project.

A tool that you could live without, but I really enjoy having just for the sheer convenience, is a heavy-duty shop vacuum cleaner. It makes quick work of cleanup and saves time in collecting stray saw dust.

TYPES OF WOOD

Rule of thumb: the harder the wood, the higher the price. When making small objects for a wall or table display, soft woods work well. Furniture and projects that will take abuse should be made from harder woods to prevent scratching and marring.

Soft wood usually comes from the pine family and is less expensive . Hard woods include oak, birch and maple. White pine is a good general purpose wood.

Wood is available in different grades, 1, 2 and 3. Grade 1 is the best and the clearest. Classification of wood is determined by its exterior appearance. It is classified as either select or common based.

Select wood is smooth and should have good grain markings. It will be a little higher priced. Common based is less expensive but may have some defects.

Common based wood will be more than suitable for most of the projects in the book. Position patterns so that any flaws are outside the pattern area. Beware of warped lumber! You can work around knots and splits, but warp is almost impossible to overcome.

How you buy your lumber is just as important as where.

The nominal size of lumber is the rough size before it is planed. For example, a 1"x 4" actually measures 3/4" x 3-1/2". The actual size of hard wood, however, is only 1/8" smaller than the nominal dimension, but there is no standard as there is in soft wood. Therefore, a hardwood 1" x 4" measures approximately 7/8" x 3-7/8".

Plywood can be used for some of the projects. It is better to use for larger pieces so no joining is necessary. Plywood is usually sold in 4' x 8' sheets, but be sure to check for smaller and miss-cuts if you only need small quantities. Plywood may also be purchased pre-sanded, so that only a light sanding will be necessary.

Particle board (a pressed wood) can also be used, but it does not finish well. So it is better to use this type of wood only in areas where it will not show.

Luan plywood is inexpensive and finishes well. For most of the patterns that call for 1/4" or thin wood, luan would probably be the best choice. Example: Luan would be a good choice for the Christmas ornaments.

Most of the patterns may be cut from either 1/2" or 3/4" pine, with thinner objects being cut from a plywood material and glued on an object to create a 3-D effect. You can choose for yourself what thickness of wood to use.

However, be aware if you cut a pattern from 3/4" wood when it calls for 1/2" wood, it will not fit together correctly. Make sure you check your wood sizes and make all necessary adjustments to the pattern before you begin.

PATTERN ENLARGEMENT AND TRANSFER

There are several different ways to transfer and enlarge patterns. You can experiment with them to see which method you feel most comfortable with.

The first type is the "grid" method. As you can see, some of the patterns in this book are laid out on a graph-paper-like grid. The grid is composed of squares, each representing a specified size. These sizes will be given on the pattern and will vary from pattern to pattern.

When you get ready to copy the pattern from the book to another sheet of paper, the first thing you need to do is to continue the lines of the grid in the book through the pattern. In other words, extend the lines of the grid through the pattern, so that the pattern has lines drawn through it.

Then get some graph paper or draw another grid on a separate piece of paper. The grid can be as large or as small as you want it to be. If you want the copied pattern to be the same size as the one in the book, make sure the grid squares on your extra piece of paper are the same size as the ones in the book. If you want to make a larger copy of the pattern, make the squares in the grid larger. When you have your grid sized the way you want, simply draw in the same lines that are in the corresponding squares on the pattern in the book.

Another way to enlarge your pattern is through the use of an instrument called a pantograph. A pantograph is an architectural tool — it looks like four long rulers joined together in a zigzag design. This tool can be difficult to work with but is very reliable. These instruments can be found in craft stores, craft catalogs and ads in woodworking magazines.

You could also check with your local newspaper office. Newspaper offices usually have enlargement machines, and they may offer pattern enlargement or reduction. The cost will vary depending upon the publisher.

You also may want to consider using photography for pattern enlargement (even though this method could become expensive). You can photograph your pattern using a 35 mm camera with slide film. Then take the developed slide and project the image directly onto a piece of wood or paper and trace it. This method has the advantage of an infinite enlargement range; however, its main drawback is the cost of film and developing.

The last and most popular method of enlargement is photocopying. Many available copiers can reduce or enlarge patterns from 50 –160%. Photocopiers may be found in many public places, including libraries, and copying is relatively inexpensive. The most obvious advantage of photocopying is that it may be used for exact pattern transfer as well as for enlargements.

When transferring a pattern to a piece of wood, use tracing paper (available at sewing centers) or carbon paper. Both work the same way. Put the pattern on top of the carbon paper. Then, place the carbon paper on the wood. Trace the pattern, and remove the paper. The image has now been transferred to the wood.

When half patterns are shown in the book (i.e., a heart shape, where each half is exactly the same), fold a piece of paper in half. Draw or trace the half pattern on the paper with the center touching the fold. Cut the pattern on the paper while folded. When opened, the pattern will be perfectly symmetrical.

HOW TO CUT YOUR PATTERN

Don't let the complexity of a pattern discourage you. Most of the cuts just need a steady hand and a little patience.

Simply break complicated cuts into simpler curves and lines. Don't be afraid to move your saw to a different position on the wood and approach the line from a different angle.

Examine each pattern before you make any cuts. Use a smaller blade to cut curves and corners if there is no way to change the position of your saw and no waste stock to cut into. (Waste stock is the extra wood around the pattern.)

If your design calls for sharp corners where two lines intersect, cut the first line and keep going past the corner. Cut a loop around in the waste stock and cut the second line. You can also cut the first line and continue cutting to the edge of the wood. Take off the waste and turn the piece; then continue cutting from the edge to the second line.

When cutting sharp interior corners, you can cut the first line up to the corner, then back the blade out of the wood and cut the second line. Another method is to cut the first line up to the corner and back up a few blade widths. Turn into the waste area (leaving the first line) and get in position to cut the second. Cut the second line and take off the waste. Then go back and cut

the last part of the second line up to the corner.

When cutting small pieces or very thin veneers, tape your wood to heavy poster board or cardboard (not corrugated cardboard). If the pieces are very thin, you can sandwich the wood between two pieces of poster board. This will prevent pieces from breaking or getting lost. It is also helpful to cut more than one thin piece at a time. This is called the pad sawing method.

Stack up the wood pieces and tape them together. The stack should not be thicker than the saw cutting capability. Saw the whole stack, then remove the tape. The pieces will be identical.

GLUING TECHNIQUES

For pieces that will be kept indoors, use a white wood glue or a yellow aliphatic resin. Outdoor projects require a waterproof glue such as resorcinol or epoxy.

Before you begin gluing, make sure the surfaces to be glued are smooth, dry and free from oil or grease. Clean surfaces take glue much easier than dirty ones.

Apply the glue, then clamp the wood together tightly. Metal or strap clamps can be used. When using metal clamps, be sure to place a padding between the clamp and your piece to prevent marring. Allow plenty of time for the glue to set and dry completely. Manufacturers usually specify drying times on the glue container.

Make certain that all glue is cleaned from the outer surfaces of pieces that you are going to stain. Stain will not absorb into any glue spots on your project.

FINISHING HOW-TO'S

How you "finish" any project is what will place your individual signature on a piece. So, decide how you want the piece to look and get to work.

Step one: Sanding the piece with a rough grade of sandpaper (100-200 grit) will knock off all large bumps and splinters. Now sand again with finer paper or emery cloth (up to 500 grit) until the piece is completely smooth. Steel wool (0000 or 4-0) is best for the final sanding and for smoothing bubbles between coats of finish or polyurethane. This is the "secret" to all those great pieces that you find in those high priced craft stores.

There are several different ways to finish the piece. It can be painted, stained, stenciled or finished with tung oil.

If painting your project, make sure you use top quality paint brushes made of camel hair or other natural fibers. These do not lose bristles and spoil the effect as cheaper made brushes do. Applicators on wooden handles are better because they don't leave brush marks. You also may use a power sprayer to get a clean, finished surface. It is always a good idea to keep several lint-free rags handy for clean up as well as for applying stains and sealers.

Acrylic paints are easy to use and easy to clean up. Plain water and soap will clean brushes thoroughly. You may decide to buy and use a brush cleaner that contains a conditioner which will help keep your brushes more supple and make them last longer. Acrylic paints, once dried on the wood surface, become permanently waterproof.

If you're feeling a little unsure about your ability to paint your projects, don't worry. You're not alone! We've found that many people who feel very comfortable with a saw in their hands suddenly feel awkward when confronted with a paint brush. For this very reason, there are many publications in craft, hobby or do-it-yourself hardware stores on painting.

The most popular type of painting for wooden pieces is tole painting. This is an easy method of applying paint in layers with common designs and shading techniques. Tole painting is probably simpler for a beginner than any other type of painting, and, with practice, patience and the proper instructions, anyone can master this technique. You'll find that a large variety of tole painting books is available in craft and hobby shops everywhere. In fact, many of the patterns included in this book already have designs suitable for tole painting.

Stenciling is another very popular finishing technique. Stenciling is the art of dabbing paint, ink or dye through openings in a piece of plastic or cardboard, leaving an impression behind. A great variety of patterns — from flowers and animals to country designs — is available.

Once you've decided on your stencil pattern, tape the pattern down to the wood surface. (You may want to practice stenciling on paper before you attempt painting on the wooden piece, just to make sure it's going to turn out the way you're hoping it will.)

The "dry brush" method of stenciling works best. Too much paint on your brush will run or drip. Use brushes, sponges or spray paint to stencil.

A new product on the market is a stick paint. Stick paints look very much like large crayons, and you "color" with them the same way you color with crayons. The stick application is very easy, and it involves less mess than other methods. It is widely becoming the favorite of many first-time stencilers.

Staining is another popular finish for wooden pieces. Color variety is an added advantage of wood stain. Just make sure you test your stain on a piece of scrap wood to check the color before putting it on the wooden piece to avoid disappointment.

Stain is easy to apply. Apply it with a brush, or wipe it on with a lint-free soft cloth. Always apply the stain with the grain of the wood, then against the grain. Wipe off the excess with the grain.

After staining, rub the piece with 0000 grit sand paper. Brush on a coat of polyurethane over the dried stain, brushing along with the grain, forcing out the bubbles. After it has dried thoroughly, follow with a steel-wool rub to eliminate any bubbles that may have formed.

For best results, use a tacky cloth (found at paint stores and most do-it-yourself hardware stores) to remove dust after each sanding. Polyurethane forms a hard, bright, waterproof finish. It comes in a high gloss or satin finish. Make sure you are in a well-ventilated, dust-free environment when applying polyurethane.

Tung oil is also a great finish. Tung oil is a thick, heavy liquid applied directly to the wood by hand or with a lint-free cloth. Several coats form a water- and stain-resistant finish. A coat of polyurethane over the dried tung oil will protect the surface even more.

OTHER THINGS YOU WILL NEED

To help make your woodworking time more enjoyable, we have included a list of optional supplies and tips to help streamline your projects. Always make certain that you have the needed lumber in the recommended sizes on hand before you start any project.

Here's a list of some additional items we recommend for getting the best results from the patterns in this book:

Plenty of sharpened #2 pencils
Twine or ribbon for enhancing certain patterns
Dowel rods of various sizes, shaker pegs
An assortment of nails, especially small finishing nails
Wood putty to cover up nail holes for finishing
Hinges and fasteners as indicated by patterns
Cup hooks, L-hooks and coat hangers — available at hardware stores
Small pliers and cutters

Whatever you decide to make and however you decide to finish it, each and every project will be very uniquely yours. Use your imagination. Combine patterns and finishing techniques. Don't be afraid to change a pattern to suit your specific needs. The joy of this book is that the patterns will become your very own creations in a short space of time. It's a great big world of woodworking fun out there — so have fun!

BRENNAN
HOUSE
est.
1954

Eagle Door Sign   1 square = 3/4"
Cut from 1/2" wood. Paint with acrylics. Coat with a light brown stain and wipe away to give the piece an antiqued look. Coat several times with polyurethane to prevent weathering. Hang beside front door. (This also could be used as a garden decoration. A hole could be drilled at the bottom and a dowel attached to insert into the ground by a gate or entrance way.)

Flower Basket Welcomer

This may be a plaque or a stand-alone welcomer. Cut out and finish with acrylic paint. Finish on both sides if it is a stand-alone piece. This would look great on or beside the front door.   **1 square = 3/4"**

Home-Sweet-Home Front Door Hanger

Cut out each piece from thin wood. Attach to rope with hot glue. If cutting from thick wood, drill holes through each piece. Tie a loop at the top to hang and a knot at the end (see diagram).

1 square = 3/4"

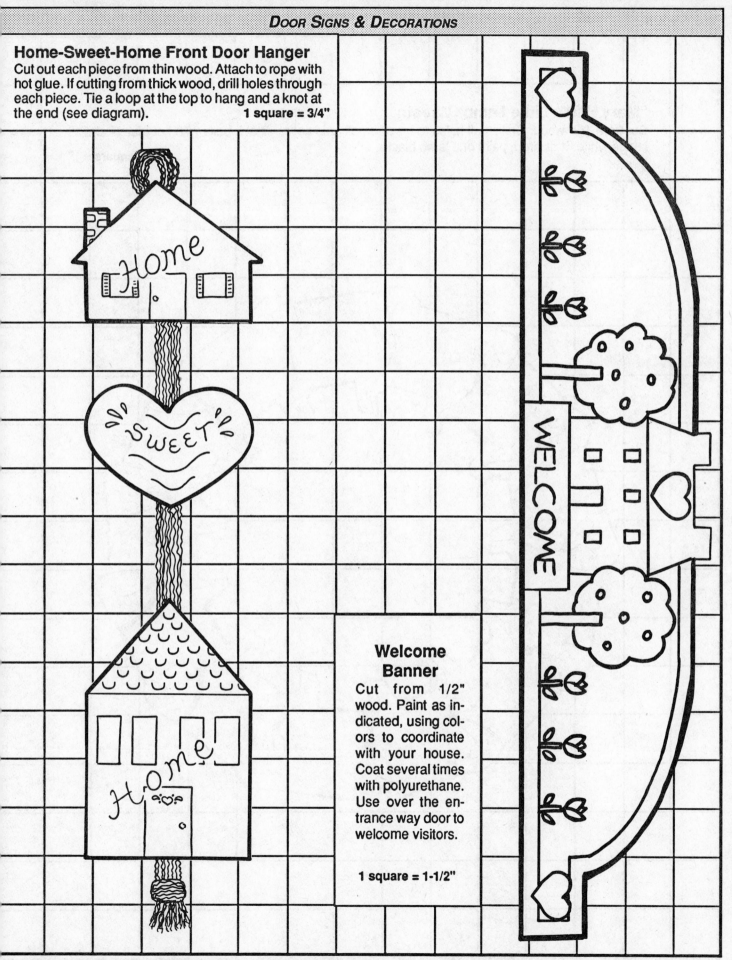

Welcome Banner

Cut from 1/2" wood. Paint as indicated, using colors to coordinate with your house. Coat several times with polyurethane. Use over the entrance way door to welcome visitors.

1 square = 1-1/2"

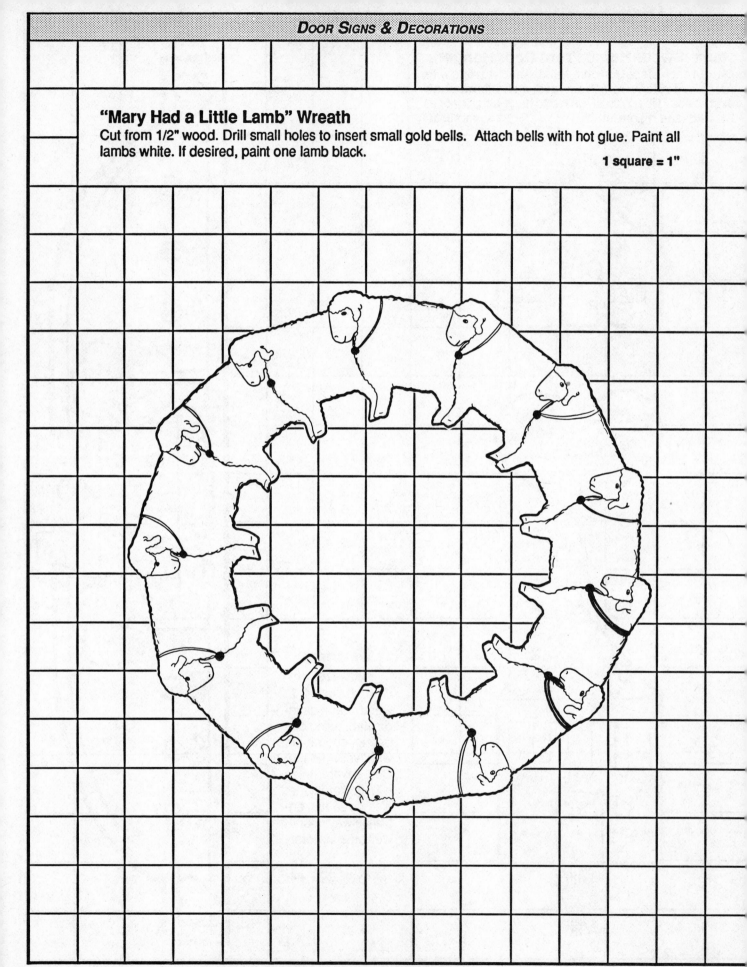

"Mary Had a Little Lamb" Wreath
Cut from 1/2" wood. Drill small holes to insert small gold bells. Attach bells with hot glue. Paint all lambs white. If desired, paint one lamb black.

1 square = 1"

American Southwestern Door Wreath with Dangling Moon   1 square = 3/4"
Cut from 1/2" wood. Cut moon from thin wood. Drill holes for fishing line or small gold twine. Paint cactus green with shading. Paint thorns black and outline each cactus. Paint coyote brown or beige with red handkerchief.

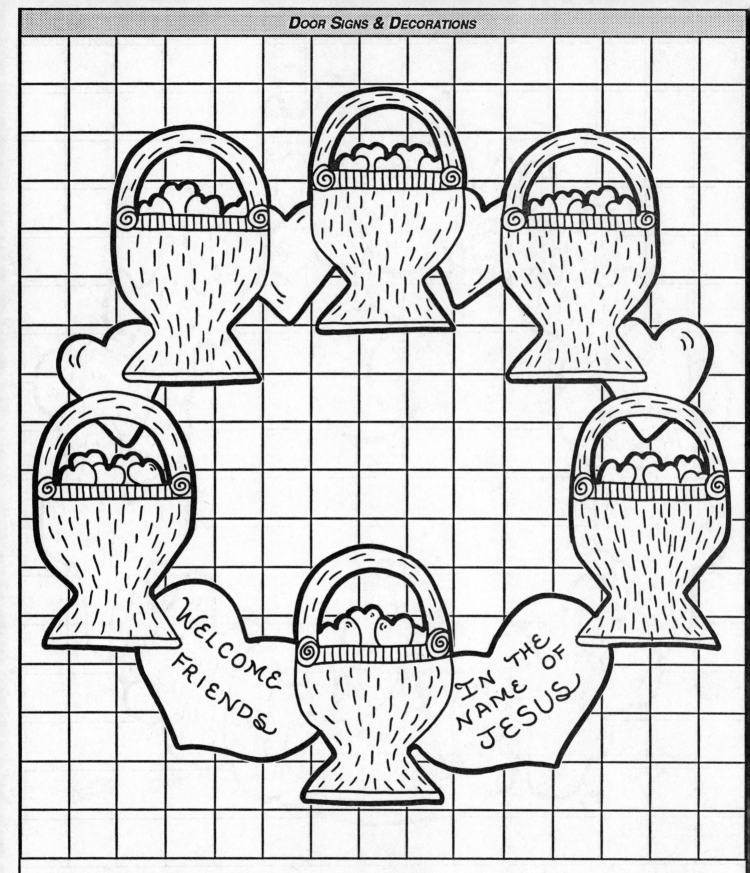

The baskets in the image contain the hand-lettered text: WELCOME FRIENDS ... IN THE NAME OF JESUS

1 square = 3/4"

"Baskets Overflowing with Hearts-of-Love" Wreath

Cut from 1/2" wood. (Baskets may be cut from luan and attached for a 3-D effect.) Paint with acrylics using red for hearts and light brown for baskets. Writing should be medium beige. Coat with clear acrylic spray.

Adobe Door Harp
Use Door Harp Instructions.

1 square = 3/4"

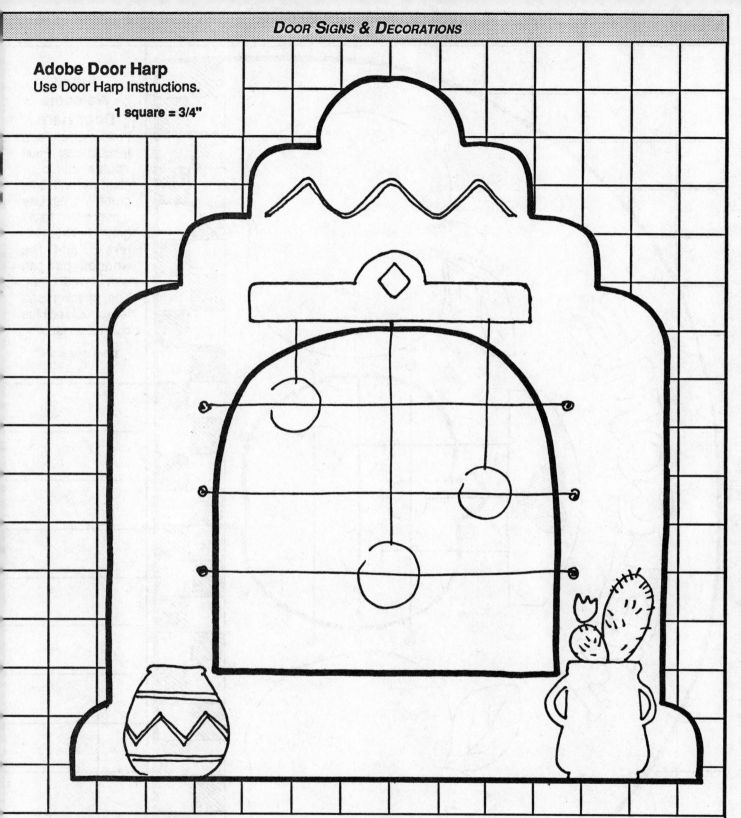

Door Harp Instructions
Cut from 1/2" to 3/4" wood and finish as shown. (These door harps do not need a back.) It would be best to purchase a door harp assembly from a do-it-yourself hardware store, craft store, or order from a woodworker's supply mail order catalog. **For do-it-yourselfers** — the quality will not necessarily be the same, but you may assemble by attaching eye hooks to string wire on. You could also purchase guitar strings and posts to mount strings. Purchase wooden balls from a hardware store. String balls on fishing line. Attach by cutting two thin wooden bars at top of harp assembly and glue together, clamping fishing line between two pieces of wood. Make sure each ball strikes wires to make a musical sound. Hang on door so that when the door is opened and closed, the harp is played.

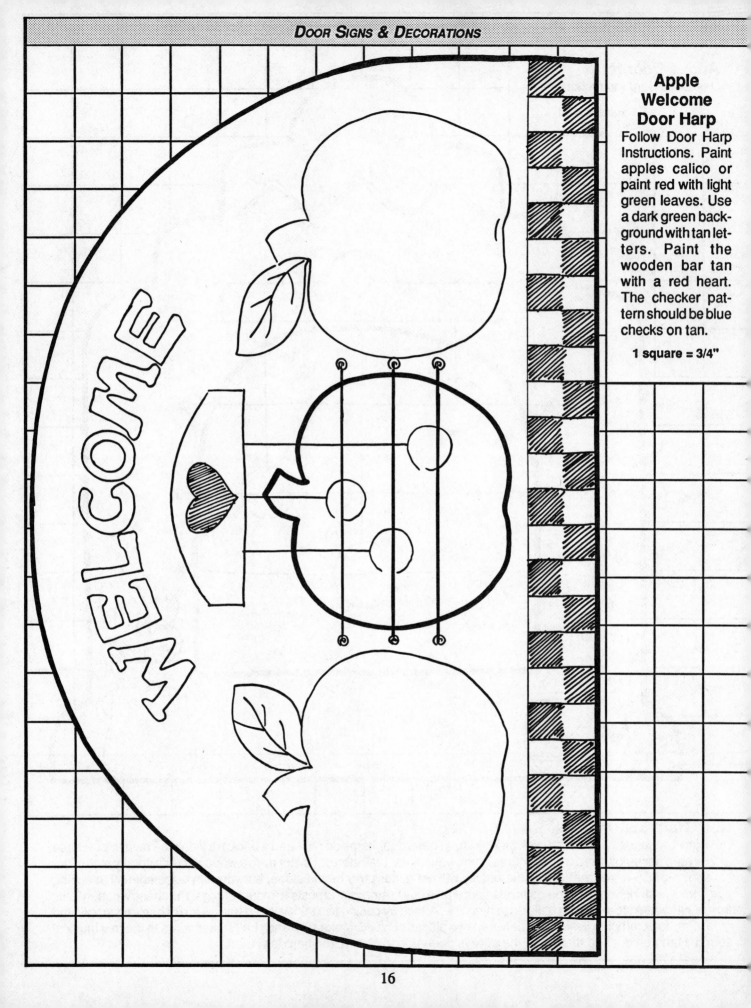

Apple Welcome Door Harp

Follow Door Harp Instructions. Paint apples calico or paint red with light green leaves. Use a dark green background with tan letters. Paint the wooden bar tan with a red heart. The checker pattern should be blue checks on tan.

1 square = 3/4"

Cow Door Harp

1 square = 3/4"

Use Door Harp Instructions. Attach a tail made from braided twine and knotted at the end.

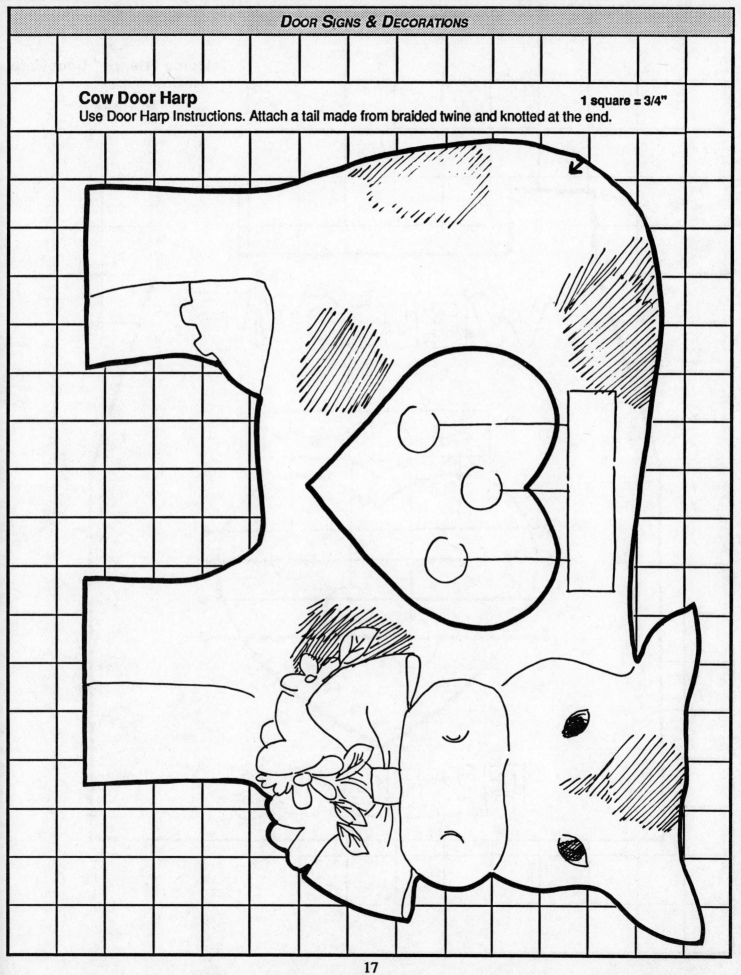

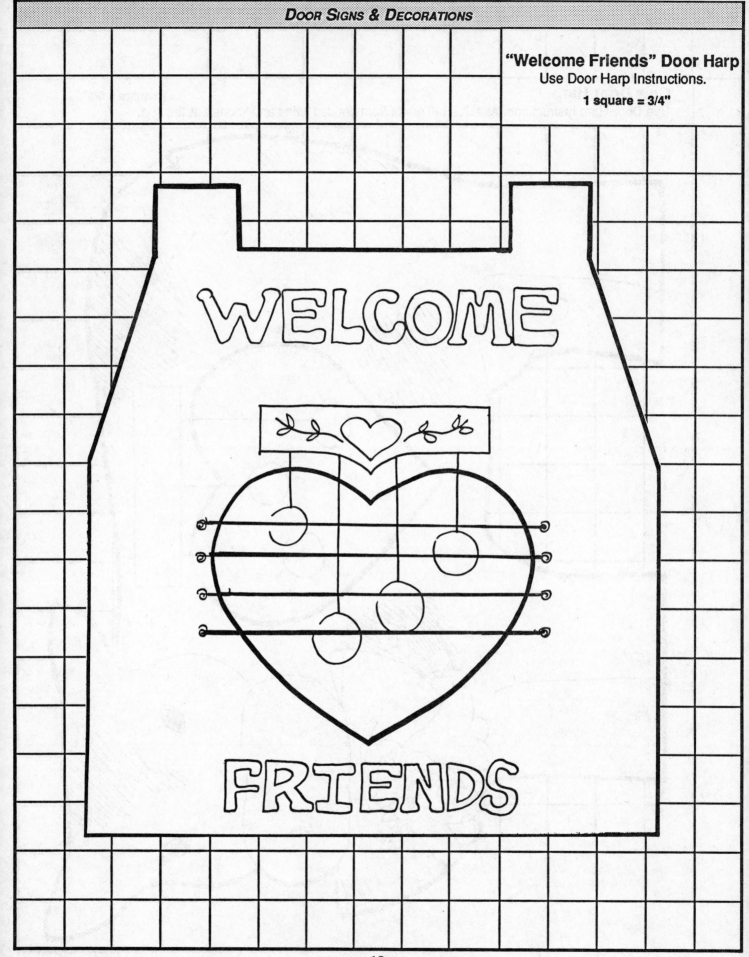

"Welcome Friends" Door Harp
Use Door Harp Instructions.
1 square = 3/4"

WELCOME

FRIENDS

Newborn Gift Plaque

Actual Size

Cut out and paint design, name and birth date. Spray with a clear acrylic finish.

APRIL SIXTH 1990

ELLEN LEIGH

Basic Directions for all Plaques

Plaques are probably the most simple and rewarding woodworking projects to do. Simply cut out the plaque, paint it using the design indicated in your choice of colors and spray with clear acrylics. Attach a hanger to the back and it's ready to use or give as a gift.

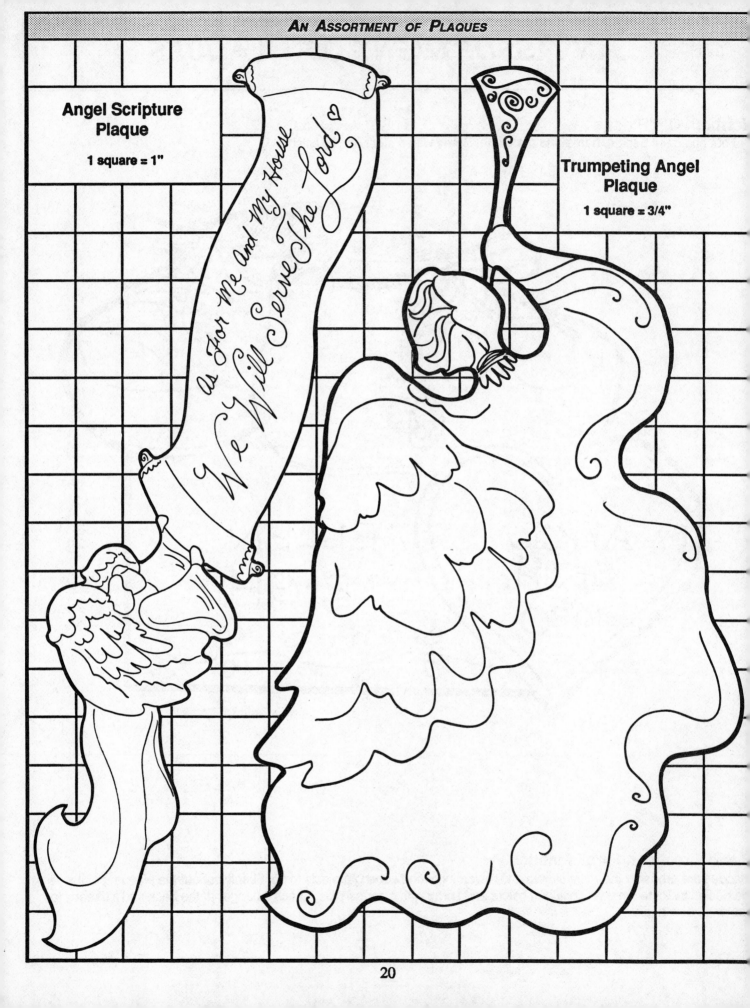

Angel Scripture Plaque

1 square = 1"

Trumpeting Angel Plaque

1 square = 3/4"

As For Me And My House We Will Serve The Lord

est. 1972

ANDERSON

Eagle Plaque
1 square = 1"

**Child's Old-Fashioned
Hobby Horse Plaque**
Cut out and drill a hole for the cord or ribbon as shown.
Finish and insert ribbon as shown. Tie a bead on the
end of the ribbon.   1 square = 3/4"

Swinging Cat and Rabbit Plaques
Cut out and drill holes as shown for thin rope. Drill holes for twine, as shown. Finish and coat with clear acrylic.

1 square = 3/4"

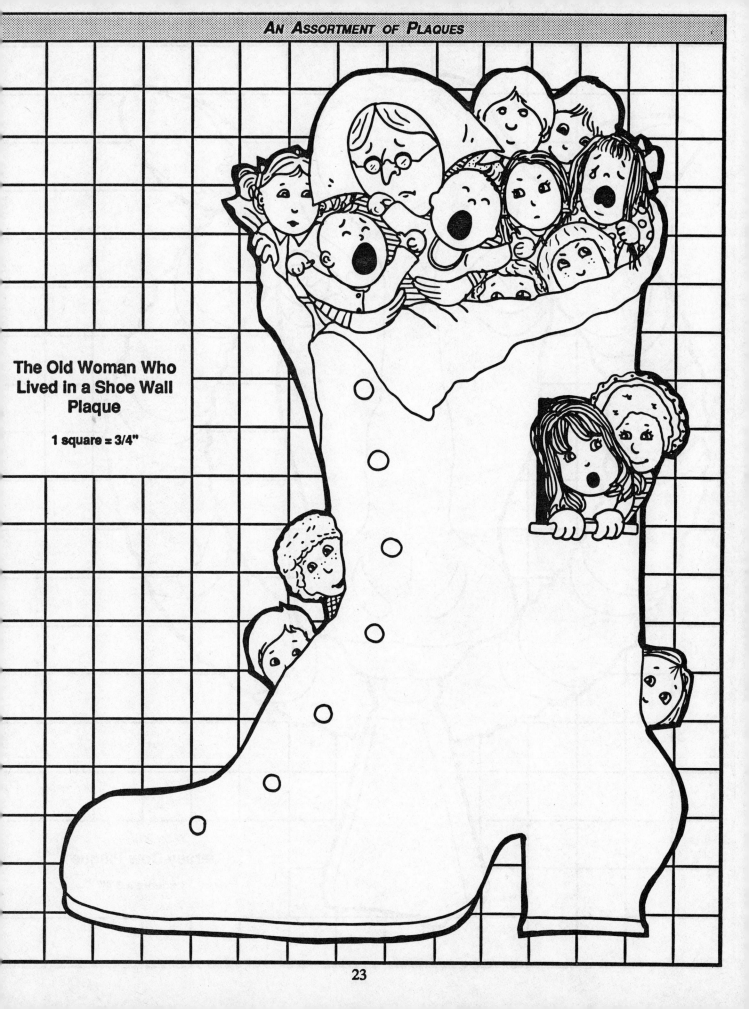

The Old Woman Who Lived in a Shoe Wall Plaque

1 square = 3/4"

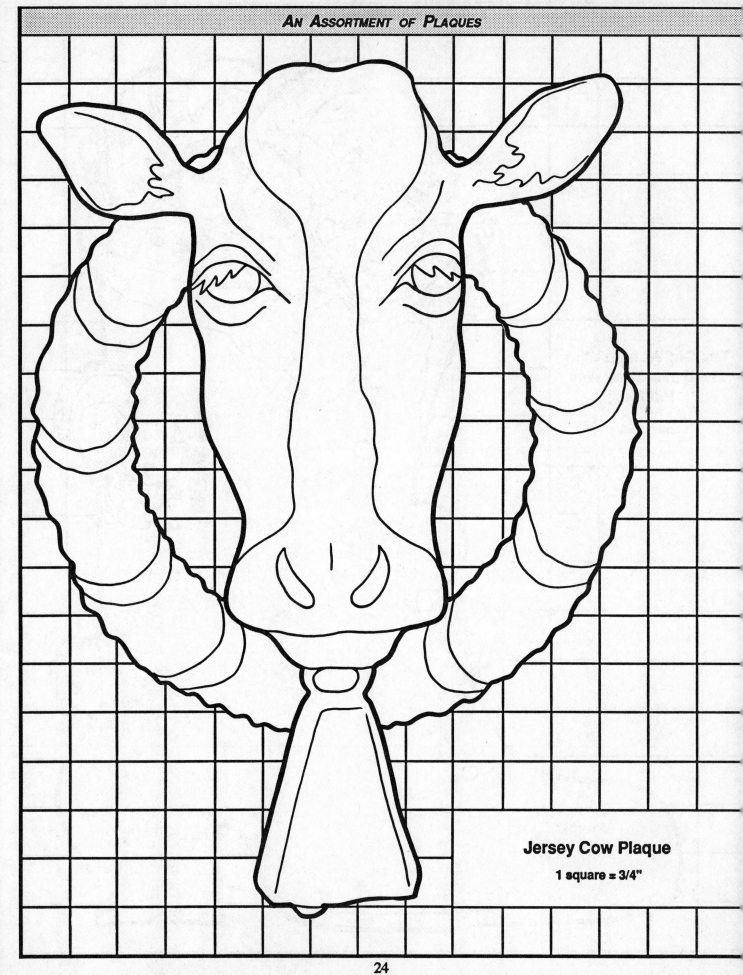

Jersey Cow Plaque

1 square = 3/4"

Wipe Your Feet Sign

Cut 1 sign from 1/2" wood. Cut woman from thin wood or luan.
Glue the woman to the sign as indicated.
Paint to coordinate with your bathroom.
Actual Size

Italian Pizza No Smoking Sign

Cut out and drill a hole as indicated for hanging. Finish with acrylics and hang with ribbon or twine.
Actual Size

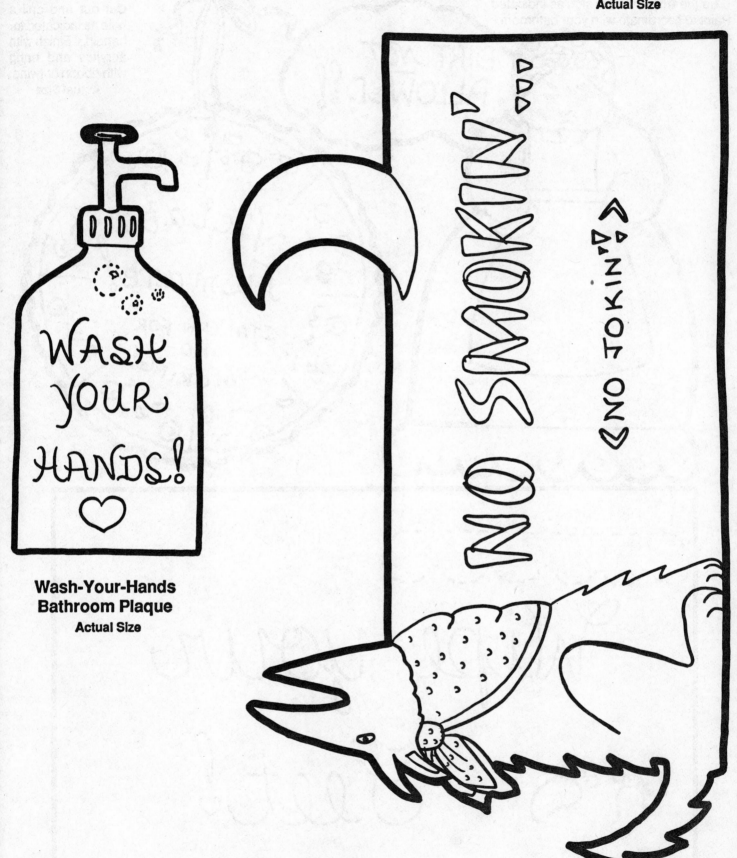

**American Southwestern
Coyote No-Smoking Sign**
Actual Size

WASH YOUR HANDS!

NO SMOKIN'

NO TOKIN'

**Wash-Your-Hands
Bathroom Plaque**
Actual Size

Clock Display Shelf

1 square = 1"

Cut 1 clock front, 1 shelf (14" long and 2" deep) and 2 brackets from 3/4" wood. Assemble using diagram. Stain or paint the clock shelf. Drill holes as indicated by X's for shaker pegs (pegs are optional). Paint on the background scene with acrylics. Use shelf for a miniature village or animals such as sheep or cows. Add the clockworks and hands according to the manufacturer's instructions.

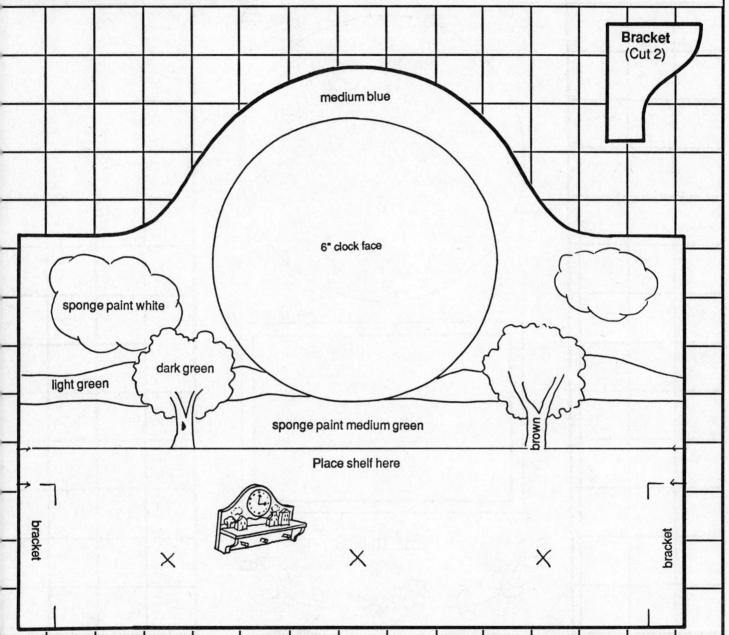

Clock Instructions

For assembly: Start by making a box for clock assembly. A back for the box is not necessary, but you may do so if desired (a pattern is not included). Glue or nail clock front to box. Clocks may be purchased from a clock shop, a craft or hobby shop, or a do-it-yourself hardware store. Assemble clock with instructions given with the clock. Clock assemblies usually come with numerals and hands. If you would prefer, or if the design is given, the numerals may be hand painted, but care must be taken to get the numbers in the correct place for the hands.

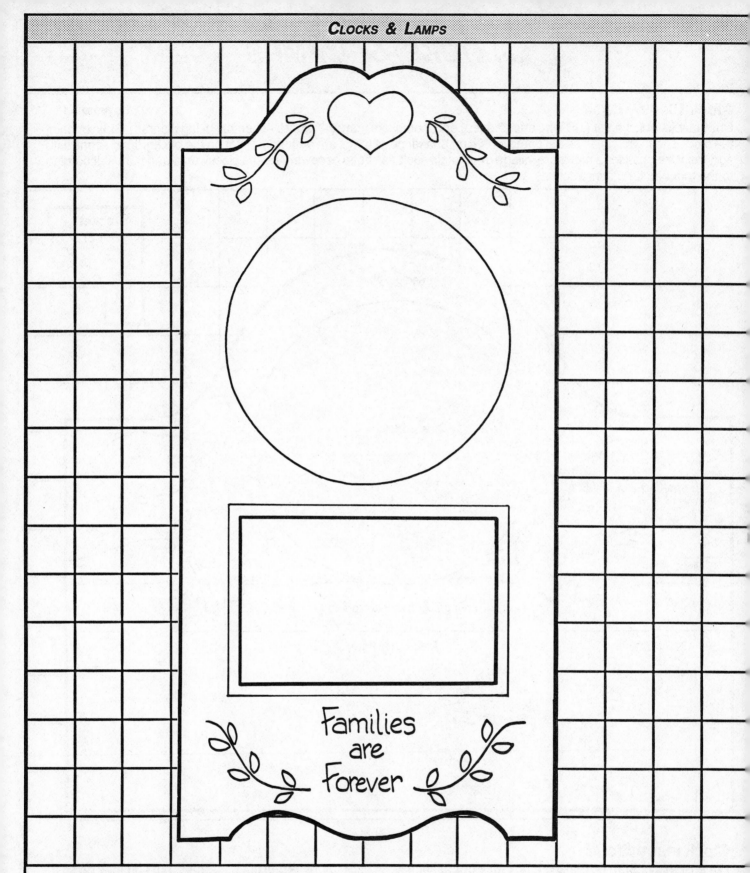

Families are Forever

Family Keepsake Photo Clock

1 square = 1"

Cut 1 clock front from 1/2" wood. Using the instructions, build a back for the clock assembly to go in. Stain or paint the clock in your choice of colors. Place a family photo in the space given after finishing. (Molding may be added around the photo if desired, and glass or plexiglass would make a good protective barrier.) Add the clockworks and hands according to the manufacturer's instructions.

American Southwestern Design Clock

1 square = 1"

Follow instructions for clock assembly on page 27. Paint design in cool desert colors, such as light beige, teal, turquoise, siennas and oranges.

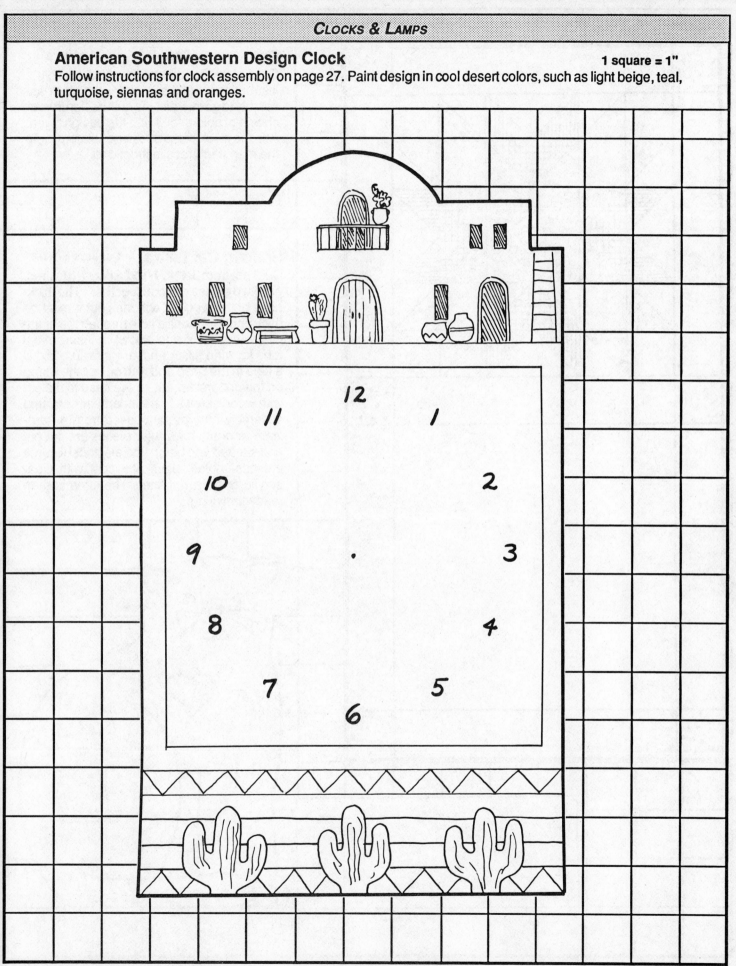

Patchwork Clock   1 square = 1"

Cut 1 clock front from 1/2" wood. Using the instructions, build a back for the clock assembly to go in. Paint the quilt design in your choice of colors following the design given. Add the clockworks and hands according to the manufacturer's instructions.

Smiling Cat Lamp   1 square = 1-1/2"

Cut 1 cat from 3/4" to 1-1/2" wood. (If desired, glue two pieces of wood together.) The thickness of the wood is optional, but it must be thick enough to drill a hole through the entire piece (from arrow to arrow) to insert metal tube for wiring. Cut 1 base. Make sure to drill a hole in the base and rout out for the wiring on the underside. Attach the base to the cat with wood screws from underneath. A lamp assembly may be purchased from a hardware or craft store. After pieces are cut out and sanded and before the electrical fixtures are assembled, paint and coat with clear acrylic or polyurethane. The lamp is then ready for wiring.

1 square = 1"

Adobe Lamp

Cut 1 adobe house piece from 3/4" to 1-1/2" wood. (If desired, glue two pieces of wood together.) The thickness of the wood is optional, but it must be thick enough to drill a hole through the entire piece (from arrow to arrow) to insert metal tube for wiring. Cut 1 base to desired size from 1-1/2" wood. Make sure to drill a hole in the base and rout out for the wiring on the underside. Attach the base to the adobe house with wood screws from underneath. A lamp assembly may be purchased from a hardware or craft store. After pieces are cut out and sanded and before the electrical fixtures are assembled, paint and coat with clear acrylic or polyurethane. The lamp is then ready for wiring.

Birdhouse Lamp

1 square = 3/4"

Cut 1 birdhouse piece from 3/4" to 1-1/2" wood. (If desired, glue two pieces of wood together.) The thickness of the wood is optional, but it must be thick enough to drill a hole through the entire piece (from arrow to arrow) to insert metal tube for wiring. Cut 1 base. Make sure to drill a hole in the base and rout out for the wiring on the underside. Drill a hole for a 3/8" dowel perch. Attach the base to the birdhouse with wood screws from underneath. A lamp assembly may be purchased from a hardware or craft store. After pieces are cut out and sanded and before the electrical fixtures are assembled, paint and coat with clear acrylic. Add Spanish moss or thatch on the "roof," if desired. The lamp is then ready for wiring.

WELCOME

Quilted Fashion Earrings
Cut 2 posts and 2 squares. Paint as indicated and coat with clear acrylic. Attach together with ribbon or chain. Glue earring backs to back of post pieces.

Quilted Jewelry Ensemble

Quilted Heart Fashion Pin
Cut 1 heart and paint as indicated. Coat with clear acrylic. Glue a pin to the back.

Scarf Slide
Cut 1 slide. Cut holes for scarf as indicated. Paint as indicated and coat with clear acrylic.

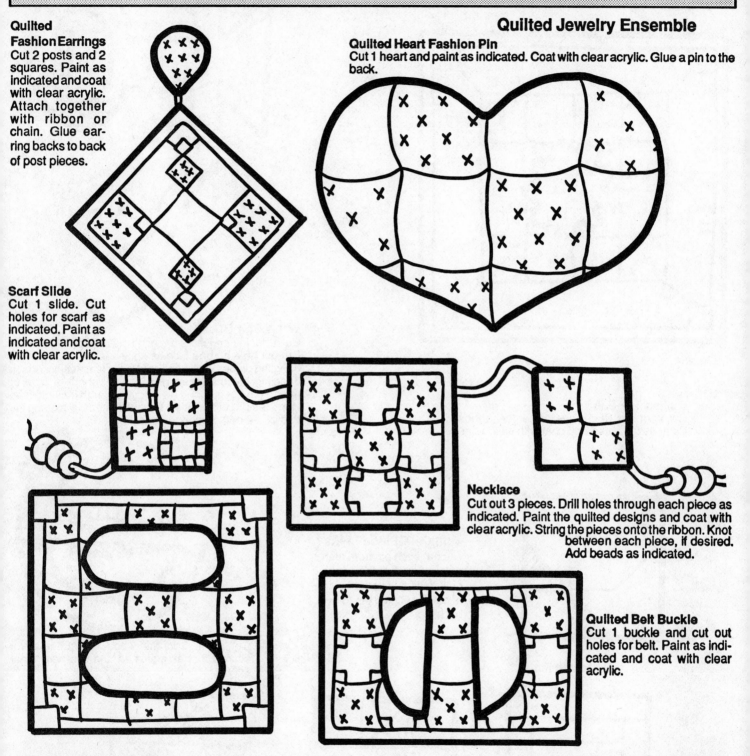

Necklace
Cut out 3 pieces. Drill holes through each piece as indicated. Paint the quilted designs and coat with clear acrylic. String the pieces onto the ribbon. Knot between each piece, if desired. Add beads as indicated.

Quilted Belt Buckle
Cut 1 buckle and cut out holes for belt. Paint as indicated and coat with clear acrylic.

Jewelry Instructions

All Jewelry Patterns are Actual Size

Cut out each piece for the individual jewelry sets. Make sure 2 earrings are cut. Turn earrings over and cut from the same patterns to insure that the earrings match. Drill holes through necklace pieces as indicated (Make sure that the hole is drilled through the top third of each piece to prevent the piece from turning.) Paint pieces on both sides (if you wish) to avoid the problems with the backs of the pieces occasionally showing. Most sets will need ribbon, beads, cord, barrettes, earring backs, and pin backs. The Tee-Slide is very popular and is used for knotting the corner edge of an oversized T Shirt. The belt buckles need to be used either with cloth belts or purchased belting. The scarf slides can be used with almost any scarf.

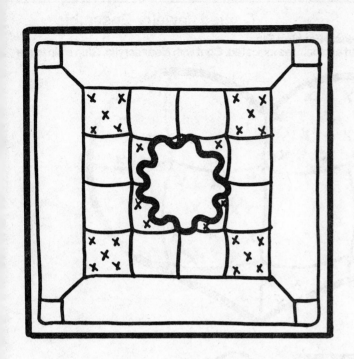

Quilted Tee-Pull

Cut 1 square. Cut hole in the center as shown. Paint as indicated and coat with clear acrylic.

Wrap Belt Buckle

Cut 1 buckle and the 2 dangling pieces from thin wood. Cut out hole on one side as shown. Drill a hole for the dangling pieces. Paint and coat with clear acrylic. Attach dangling pieces. Measure a double length of cord or ribbon (do not cut). Tie a slip knot through the hole (see Hopi Design Belt Buckle). The belt fastens by looping the end of the belt around the buckle.

Amish "Quilted" Pins

Cut out each pin from luan or thin wood. Paint on the quilt design in your choice of colors. Glue a pin to the back.

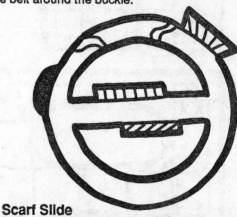

Buttercup Pin

Scarf Slide

Cut 1 slide from thin wood. Cut out holes for scarf. Paint as indicated and coat with clear acrylic.

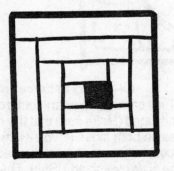

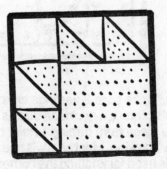

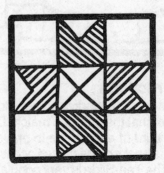

Log Cabin Pin

Bear's Paw Pin

Ohio Star Pin

Necklace

Cut out each piece. Drill holes as indicated to string on ribbon or cord. Drill small holes through middle circle piece to string narrow cord through. Paint as indicated and coat with clear acrylic spray. Make indentations in the top, inside of the middle circle piece with a small nail to insert cord and glue to top piece. Thread the cord through the small drilled holes in the bottom of circle. Make indentations in the dangling pieces and glue to the end of the cord.

Dangling Lapel Pin

Cut out lapel piece and dangling piece. Paint and coat with clear acrylic. Attach with small cord and glue as the other dangling pieces.

Dangling Earring

Follow directions for broach and lapel pin. Glue earring posts to back.

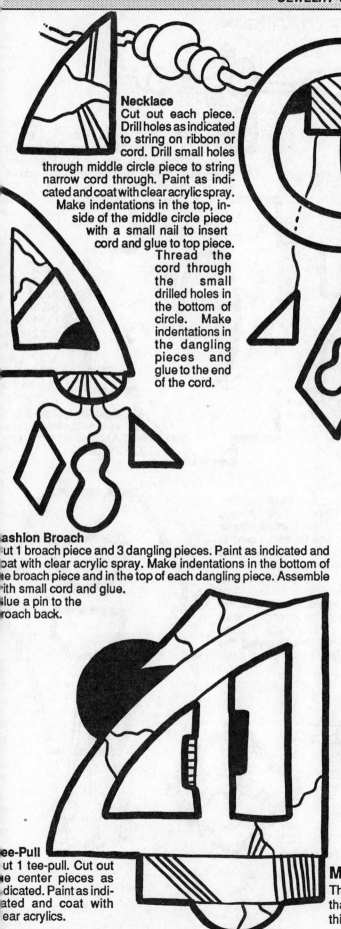

ashion Broach

ut 1 broach piece and 3 dangling pieces. Paint as indicated and oat with clear acrylic spray. Make indentations in the bottom of e broach piece and in the top of each dangling piece. Assemble ith small cord and glue. lue a pin to the roach back.

Barrette Cover
(Follow directions for barrette covers.)

Conventional Belt Buckle

Cut 1 buckle. Cut out the center pieces as indicated. Paint as indicated and coat with clear acrylic.

ee-Pull

ut 1 tee-pull. Cut out e center pieces as dicated. Paint as indi- ated and coat with ear acrylics.

Modern Jewelry with an American Indian Flair

This jewelry ensemble will not be easy to complete, but the compliments that you receive will make it worthwhile. Cut all pieces from thin wood (use thicker wood on the pieces that must be strung onto ribbon or cord).

American Hopi Indian Jewelry Ensemble

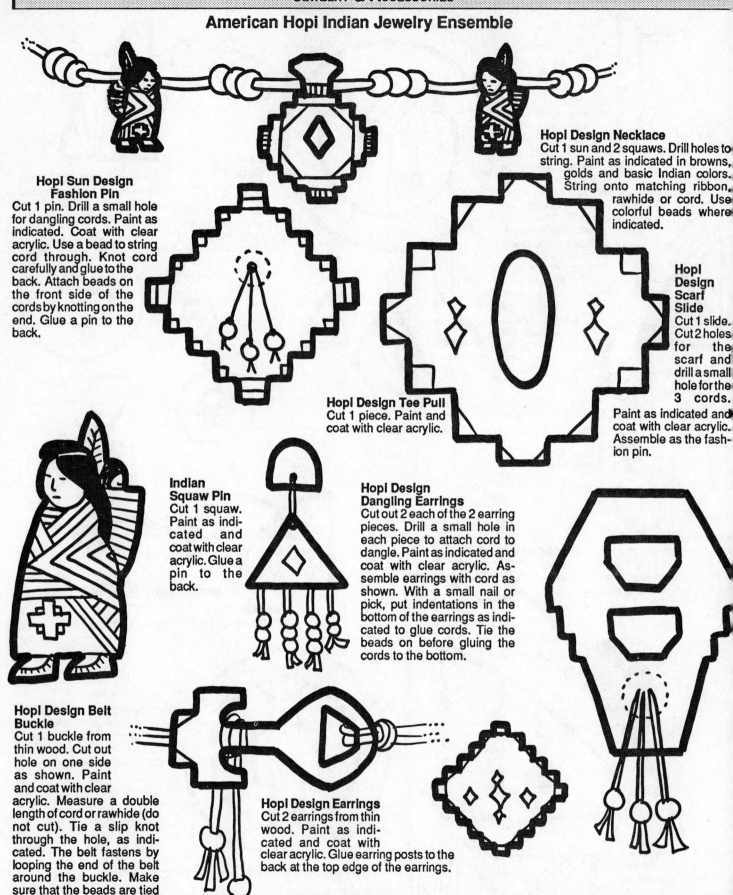

Hopi Sun Design Fashion Pin

Cut 1 pin. Drill a small hole for dangling cords. Paint as indicated. Coat with clear acrylic. Use a bead to string cord through. Knot cord carefully and glue to the back. Attach beads on the front side of the cords by knotting on the end. Glue a pin to the back.

Hopi Design Necklace

Cut 1 sun and 2 squaws. Drill holes to string. Paint as indicated in browns, golds and basic Indian colors. String onto matching ribbon, rawhide or cord. Use colorful beads where indicated.

Hopi Design Scarf Slide

Cut 1 slide. Cut 2 holes for the scarf and drill a small hole for the 3 cords. Paint as indicated and coat with clear acrylic. Assemble as the fashion pin.

Hopi Design Tee Pull

Cut 1 piece. Paint and coat with clear acrylic.

Indian Squaw Pin

Cut 1 squaw. Paint as indicated and coat with clear acrylic. Glue a pin to the back.

Hopi Design Dangling Earrings

Cut out 2 each of the 2 earring pieces. Drill a small hole in each piece to attach cord to dangle. Paint as indicated and coat with clear acrylic. Assemble earrings with cord as shown. With a small nail or pick, put indentations in the bottom of the earrings as indicated to glue cords. Tie the beads on before gluing the cords to the bottom.

Hopi Design Belt Buckle

Cut 1 buckle from thin wood. Cut out hole on one side as shown. Paint and coat with clear acrylic. Measure a double length of cord or rawhide (do not cut). Tie a slip knot through the hole, as indicated. The belt fastens by looping the end of the belt around the buckle. Make sure that the beads are tied to the end of the belt buckle.

Hopi Design Earrings

Cut 2 earrings from thin wood. Paint as indicated and coat with clear acrylic. Glue earring posts to the back at the top edge of the earrings.

Barrette Covers
Cut 2 each from thin wood. Finish with acrylic paints. Coat with clear acrylic spray. Purchase barrettes from craft or discount stores. Attach with hot glue or tacky glue. (If desired, a pin could be glued to the back to make lots of cute and seasonal bar pins for gifts.)

Watermelon Barrette

Cute Kitty Barrette

MEOW

Quilted Barrette

Koala Bear Barrette

Beaded Barrette Cover
Drill a hole as indicated for ribbons. Knot beads onto the ends as shown.

School Ruler Barrette
(Paint Yellow)

1   2   3   4

#2

Pencil Barrette

Humpty Dumpty Jewelry Ensemble

Humpty Dumpty Necklace
Cut out 3 necklace pieces. Drill holes through each piece as indicated. Paint and coat with clear acrylic spray. String the pieces onto the ribbon. Knot between each piece, if desired. Add beads as indicated.

Cracked Egg Tee-Pull
Cut 1 piece. Cut out center for t-shirt. Paint and coat with clear acrylic.

Humpty Dumpty's Derby Earrings
Cut 2 earrings. Paint and coat with clear acrylic spray. Glue earring backs on with hot glue or tacky glue.

Humpty Dumpty Fashion Pin
Cut 1. Paint as indicated and coat with clear acrylic. Glue a pin to the back.

Humpty Dumpty Barrette Cover
(Follow directions for barrette covers.)

Humpty Dumpty's Wall Scarf Slide
Cut 1 piece. Cut holes for scarf. Paint and coat with clear acrylic spray.

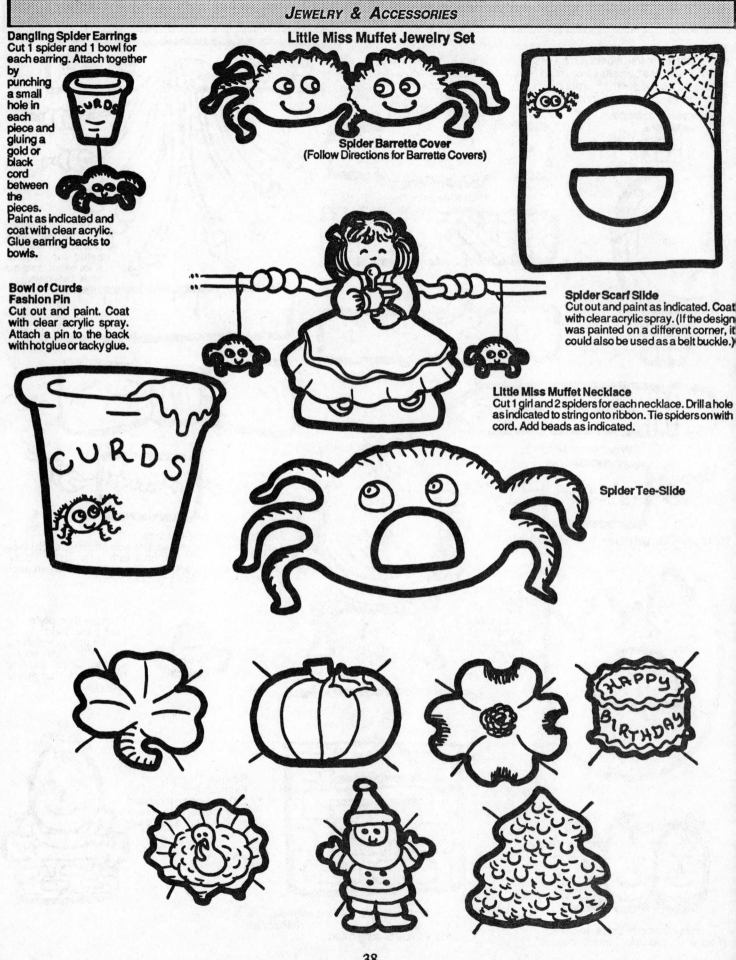

Little Miss Muffet Jewelry Set

Dangling Spider Earrings
Cut 1 spider and 1 bowl for each earring. Attach together by punching a small hole in each piece and gluing a gold or black cord between the pieces. Paint as indicated and coat with clear acrylic. Glue earring backs to bowls.

Bowl of Curds Fashion Pin
Cut out and paint. Coat with clear acrylic spray. Attach a pin to the back with hot glue or tacky glue.

Spider Barrette Cover
(Follow Directions for Barrette Covers)

Spider Scarf Slide
Cut out and paint as indicated. Coat with clear acrylic spray. (If the design was painted on a different corner, it could also be used as a belt buckle.)

Little Miss Muffet Necklace
Cut 1 girl and 2 spiders for each necklace. Drill a hole as indicated to string onto ribbon. Tie spiders on with cord. Add beads as indicated.

Spider Tee-Slide

38

"Goldilocks & The Three Bears" Jewelry Ensemble

Goldilocks' Necklace
Cut out 3 necklace pieces. Drill holes through each piece as indicated. Paint and coat with clear acrylic spray. String the pieces onto the ribbon. Knot between each piece, if desired. Add beads as indicated.

Baby Bear's Bed Tee-Pull
Cut 1 piece. Cut out center for T-shirt. Paint and coat with clear acrylic.

Papa Bear Fashion Pin
Cut 1 bear. Paint as indicated and coat with clear acrylic. Glue a pin to the back.

Three Bears Barrette Cover
(Follow directions for barrette covers.)

Mama Bear Earrings
Cut 2 bear heads. Paint and coat with clear acrylic spray. Glue earring backs on with hot glue or tacky glue.

Scarf Slide
Cut 1 piece. Cut holes for scarf. Paint and coat with clear acrylic spray.

Canvas & Athletic Shoe-Topper Instructions

Cut 2 shoe motifs (1 for each shoe). Drill holes in a cross pattern to thread the shoelaces. Sand well. Paint with acrylics in bright colors and coat with clear acrylics.

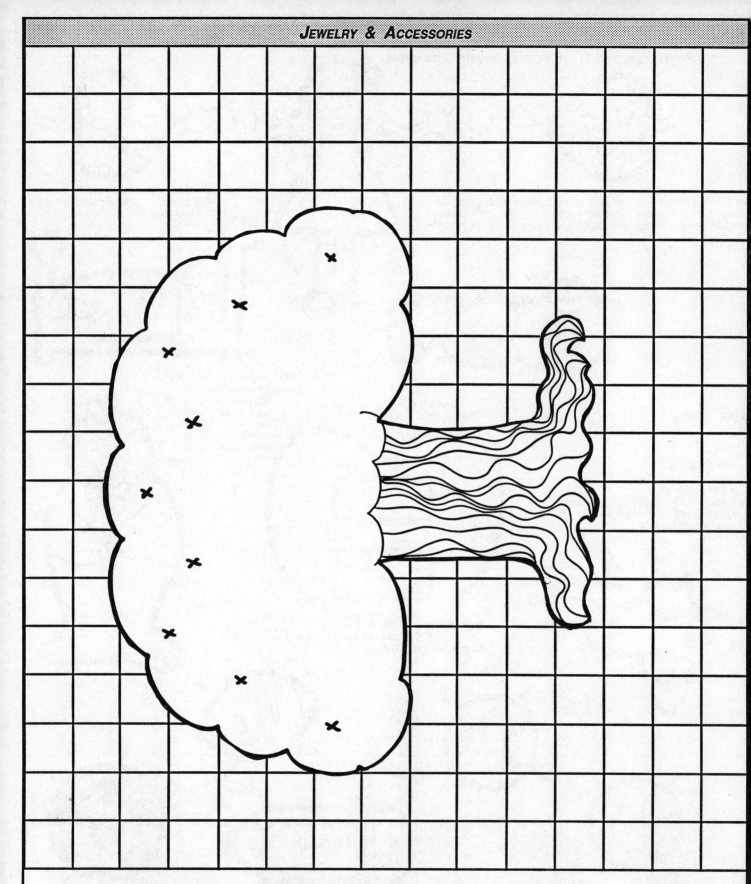

Fashion Jewelry Tree

1 square = 1"

Cut out and paint. The wavy lines on the trunk may be painted on or wood burned on. Attach L-hooks or cup hooks in the spaces indicated by X's.

PEG RACKS & PEG HANGERS

Heart Single Peg Rack
Actual Size

Peg Rack Directions

Cut out peg rack from 1/2" to 3/4" wood. (Follow any special instructions given with individual pattern.) Drill holes for pegs (if using pegs), as indicated by an X. Paint the rack with acrylic paint as shown. (Don't forget to paint the pegs.) Using wood glue, secure the pegs in the holes. Coat with clear acrylic or polyurethane. Attach a hanger to the back of the finished peg rack. There are many different types of pegs that may be used.

1. Shaker pegs are the easiest and most popular and they come in a variety of sizes. Simply drill a hole and insert the peg. Secure with wood glue.
2. Short lengths of dowel may also be used. If using dowels, drill holes in peg rack at an angle. Cut dowels and insert into holes, secure with wood glue.
3. Cup hooks or L-hooks may be purchased to screw into spaces marked.
4. Metal hooks may be purchased and fastened in place with wood screws that are usually provided with the hooks.

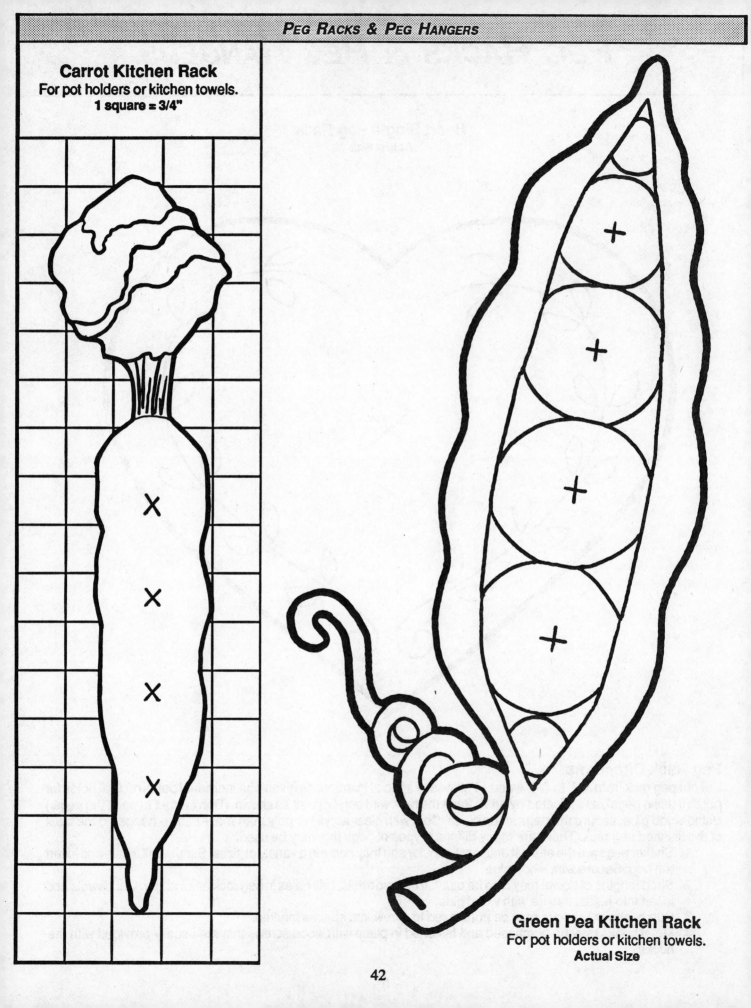

Carrot Kitchen Rack
For pot holders or kitchen towels.
1 square = 3/4"

Green Pea Kitchen Rack
For pot holders or kitchen towels.
Actual Size

Peace Coat Rack
1 square = 1-1/2"

PEACE TO ALL WHO ENTER HERE

Gaggle of Geese Peg Rack
Paint geese white. Use primary or country colors on the rest of the plaque.
1 square = 1"

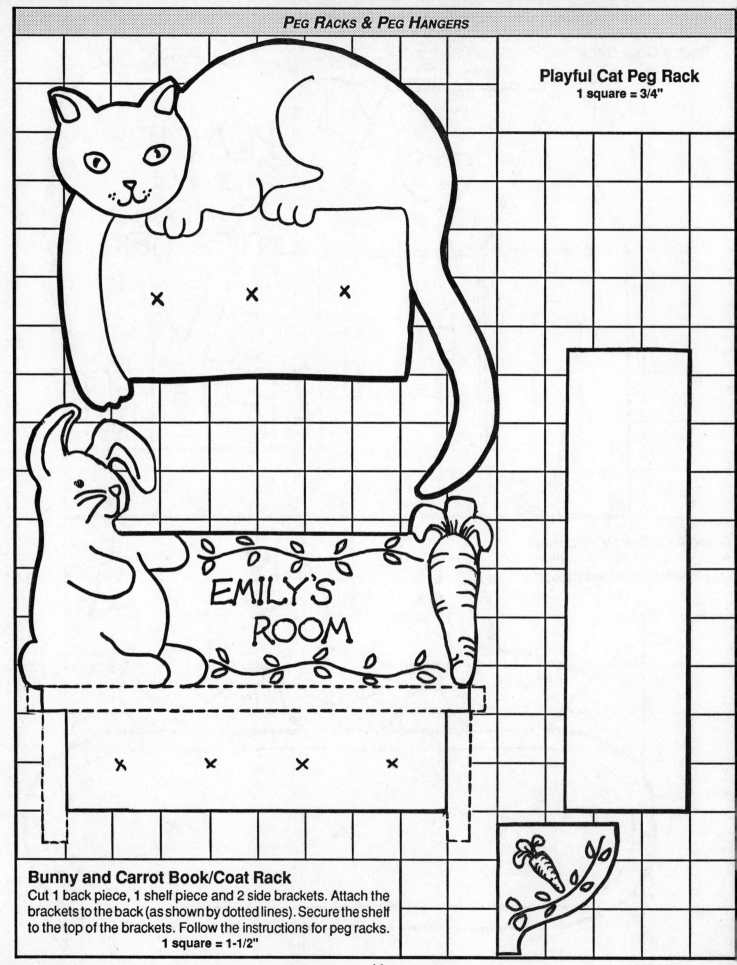

Playful Cat Peg Rack
1 square = 3/4"

EMILY'S
ROOM

Bunny and Carrot Book/Coat Rack
Cut 1 back piece, 1 shelf piece and 2 side brackets. Attach the brackets to the back (as shown by dotted lines). Secure the shelf to the top of the brackets. Follow the instructions for peg racks.
1 square = 1-1/2"

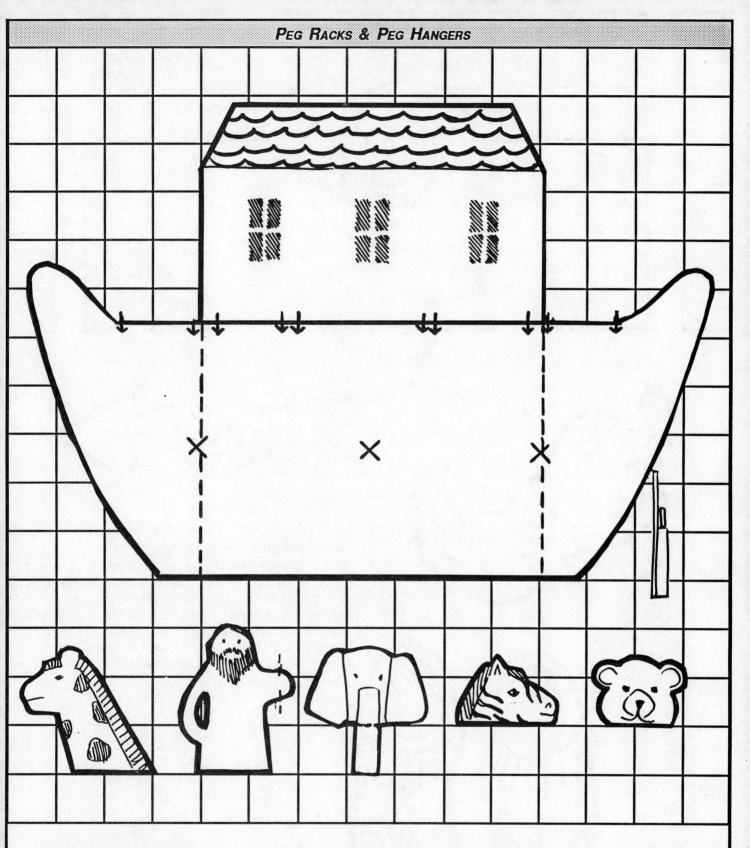

Noah's Ark Peg Rack

Cut 1 ark back (include dotted lines) from thin wood, cut 1 ark bottom from 1/2" wood. Cut 1 each of the elephant (trunk may be cut separately), zebra, giraffe, bear and Noah, from thin wood. See diagram to assemble. Follow the directions for peg racks. Noah and animal figures will appear to be looking out over the sides of the boat.

1 square = 3/4"

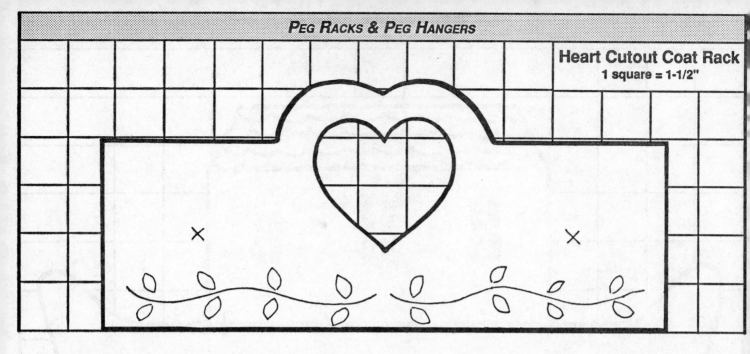

Heart Cutout Coat Rack
1 square = 1-1/2"

Southwestern Peg Hangers
Cut 2 of each design (except for moccasins) from 1/2" wood. Drill a hole in the top of each piece (as indicated by an arrow). Glue a length of sisal twine between each piece so that it may hang from pegs. (Chair-back hangers and canvas or athletic shoe-toppers may also be used for peg hangers. Check the index for page numbers.)

Actual Size

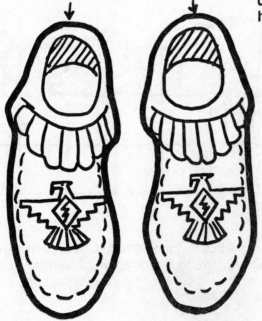

Primitive Girl Frame

Basket Frame

Tea Pot Frame

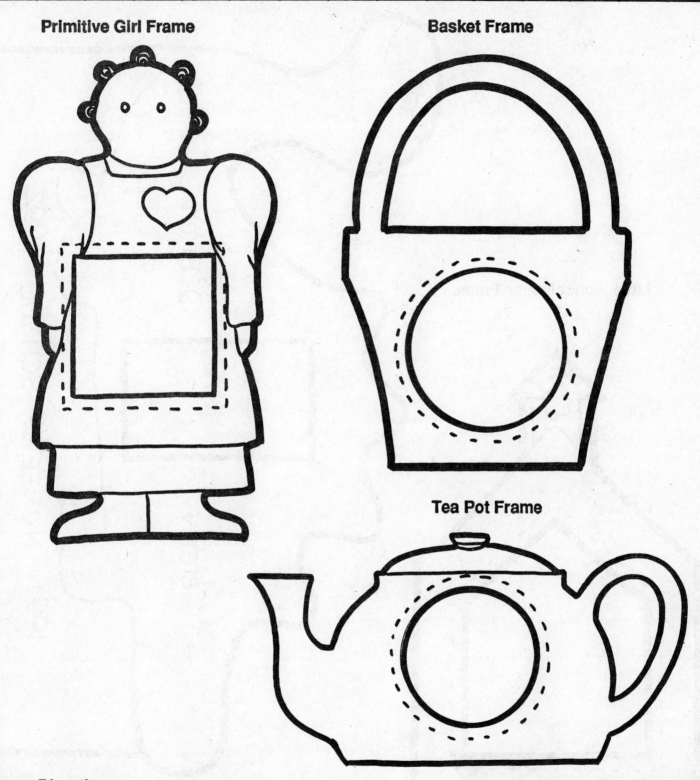

Frame Directions

All frames are actual size.

Cut 1 frame and 1 thin piece of wood from the frame pattern. Or, if you prefer, a small piece of thin wood or heavy cardboard may be cut just larger than the picture (or object to be framed) and glued to the back with the photo. If cut from thick wood, these frames will stand alone or hang, or you can purchase a stand. Use these frames for photos, snapshots or needlecraft pieces. These frames are actual size, they may be enlarged, if desired.

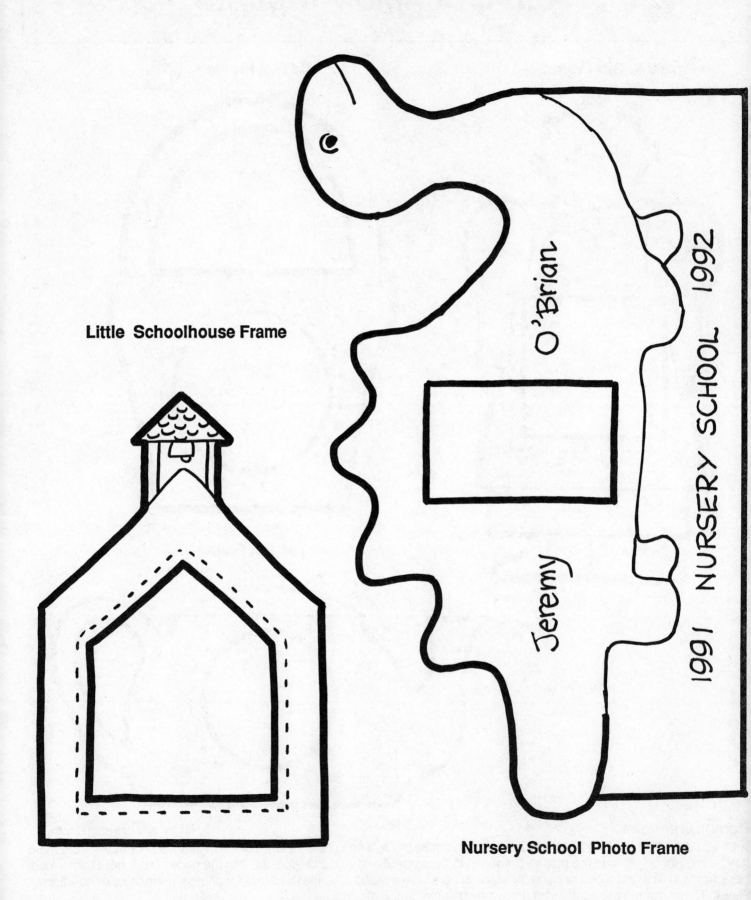

Little Schoolhouse Frame

O'Brian

Jeremy

1991 NURSERY SCHOOL 1992

Nursery School Photo Frame

Cat Frame

Home-Sweet-Home Frame

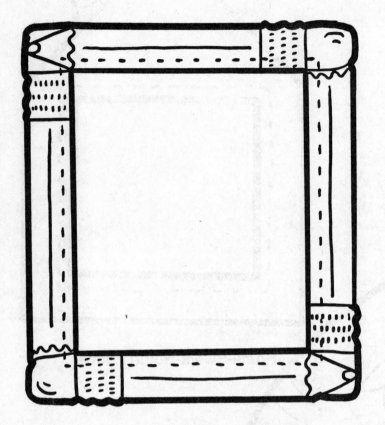

Pencil School Photo Frame

Pig Frame

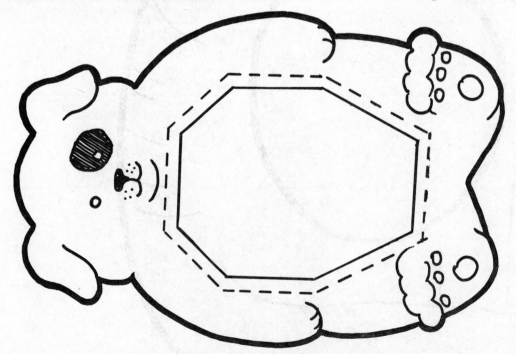

Precious Puppy Pet Frame

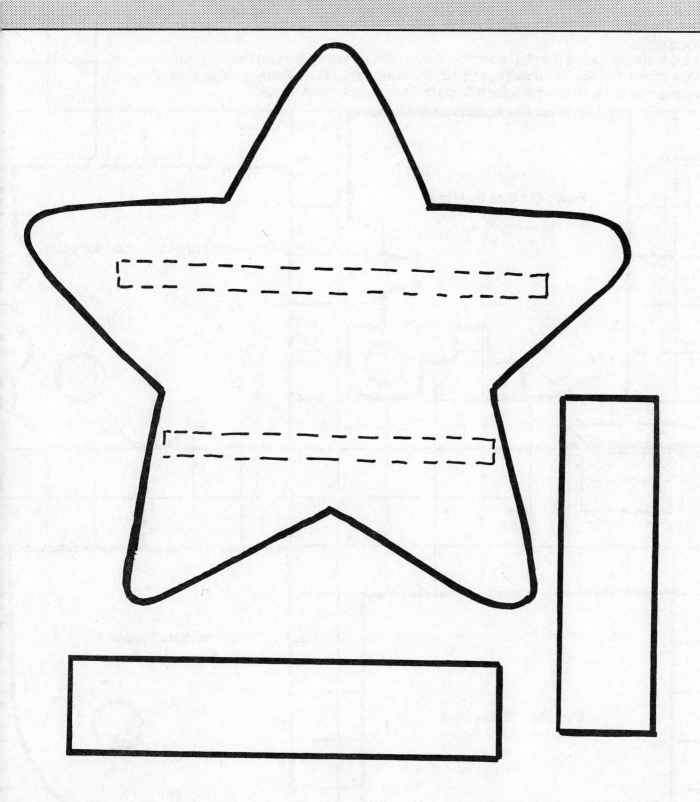

Actual Size

Star Shelf
Use for miniatures. Cut 1 star, 1 top shelf and 1 bottom shelf. Assemble (dotted lines show placement of shelves) using wood screws or small finishing nails. Attach hanger. This piece may be stained or painted.

51

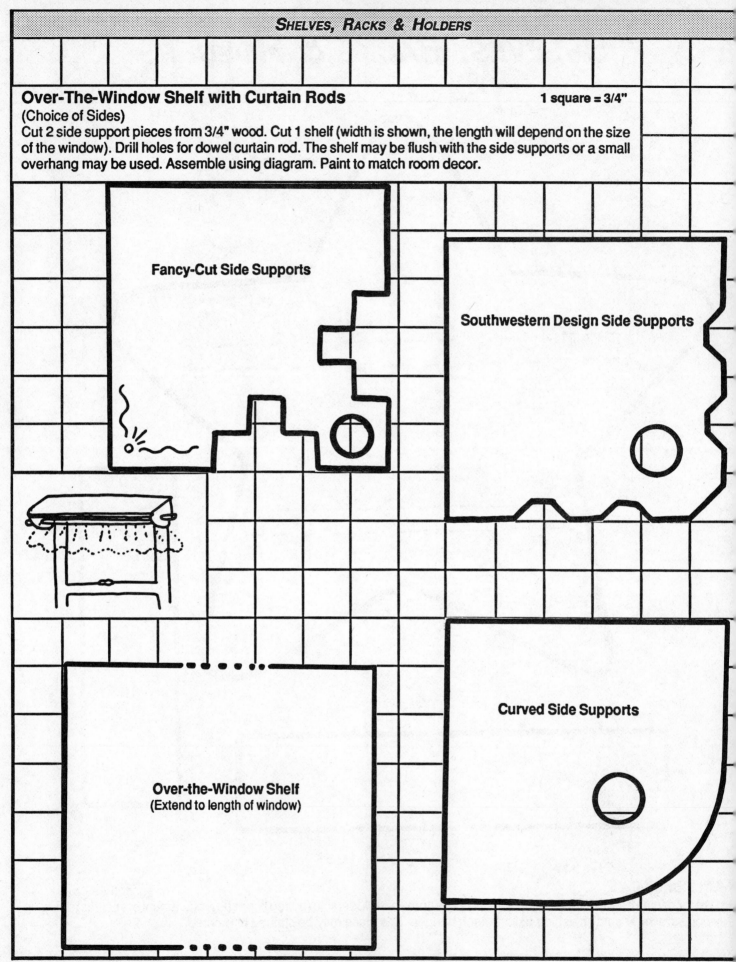

Over-The-Window Shelf with Curtain Rods

(Choice of Sides)

Cut 2 side support pieces from 3/4" wood. Cut 1 shelf (width is shown, the length will depend on the size of the window). Drill holes for dowel curtain rod. The shelf may be flush with the side supports or a small overhang may be used. Assemble using diagram. Paint to match room decor.

1 square = 3/4"

Fancy-Cut Side Supports

Southwestern Design Side Supports

Over-the-Window Shelf
(Extend to length of window)

Curved Side Supports

SHELVES, RACKS & HOLDERS

52

Dollhouse Shadow Box Display Case

1 square = 1-1/2"

Cut all pieces (except stairs) from 1/2" wood. Cut 1 back piece, 2 side pieces, 3 shelves (floors) and 1 divider. Cut 1 set of stairs from 1-1/2" wood. Assemble, using the diagram. Paint designs as shown. Wallpaper may be used in the "rooms". This could also be used as a dollhouse.

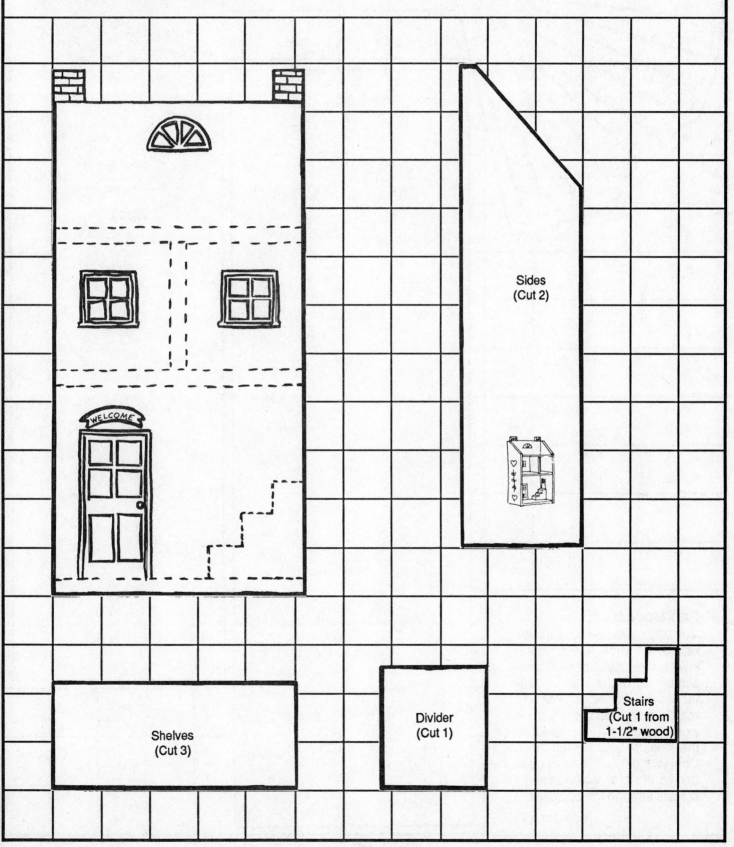

Sides
(Cut 2)

Shelves
(Cut 3)

Divider
(Cut 1)

Stairs
(Cut 1 from
1-1/2" wood)

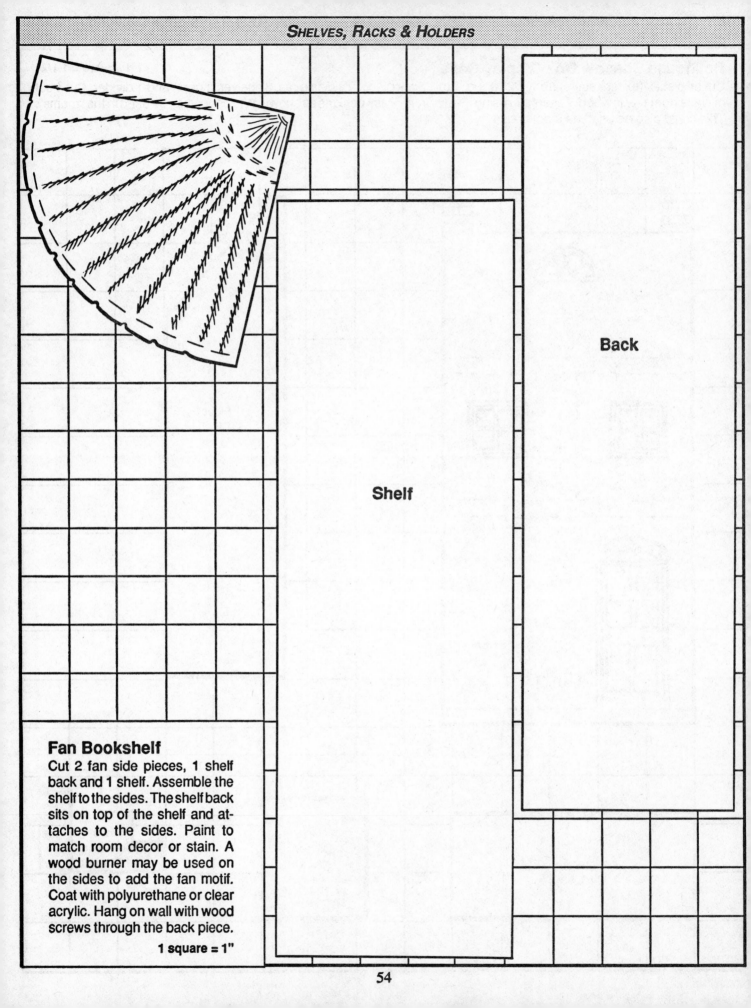

Back

Shelf

Fan Bookshelf

Cut 2 fan side pieces, 1 shelf back and 1 shelf. Assemble the shelf to the sides. The shelf back sits on top of the shelf and attaches to the sides. Paint to match room decor or stain. A wood burner may be used on the sides to add the fan motif. Coat with polyurethane or clear acrylic. Hang on wall with wood screws through the back piece.

1 square = 1"

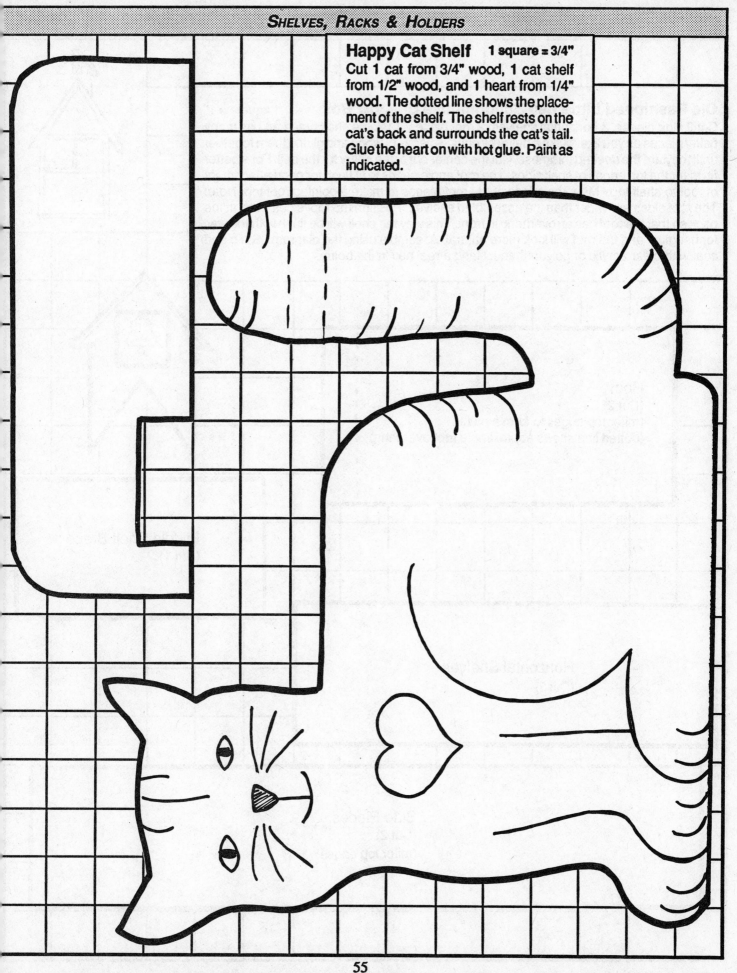

Happy Cat Shelf   **1 square = 3/4"**
Cut 1 cat from 3/4" wood, 1 cat shelf from 1/2" wood, and 1 heart from 1/4" wood. The dotted line shows the placement of the shelf. The shelf rests on the cat's back and surrounds the cat's tail. Glue the heart on with hot glue. Paint as indicated.

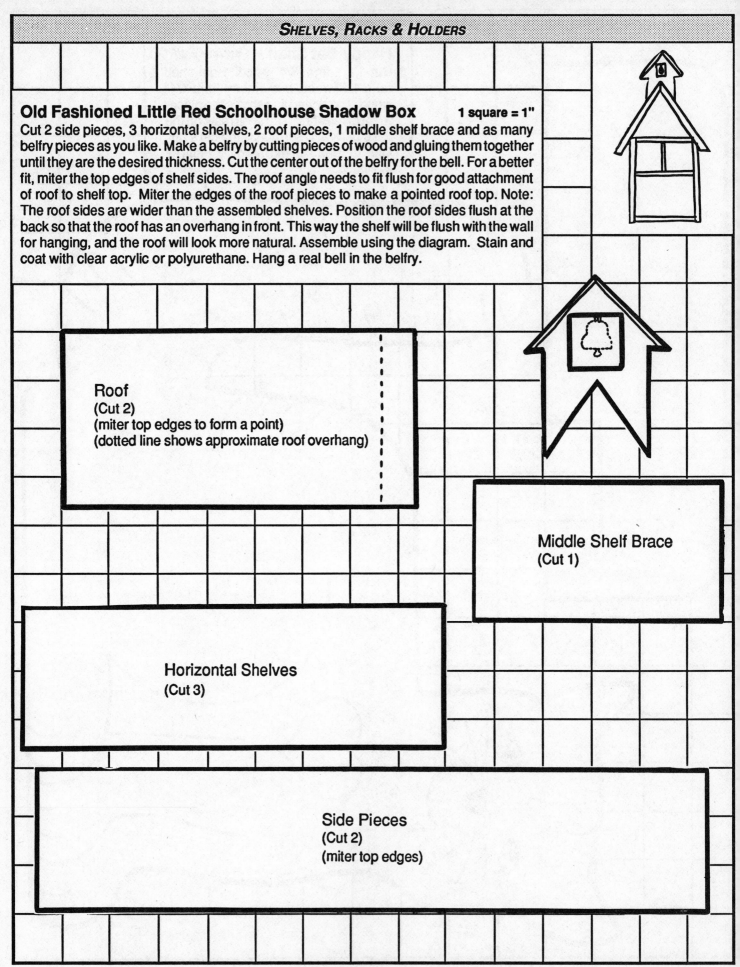

Old Fashioned Little Red Schoolhouse Shadow Box

1 square = 1"

Cut 2 side pieces, 3 horizontal shelves, 2 roof pieces, 1 middle shelf brace and as many belfry pieces as you like. Make a belfry by cutting pieces of wood and gluing them together until they are the desired thickness. Cut the center out of the belfry for the bell. For a better fit, miter the top edges of shelf sides. The roof angle needs to fit flush for good attachment of roof to shelf top. Miter the edges of the roof pieces to make a pointed roof top. Note: The roof sides are wider than the assembled shelves. Position the roof sides flush at the back so that the roof has an overhang in front. This way the shelf will be flush with the wall for hanging, and the roof will look more natural. Assemble using the diagram. Stain and coat with clear acrylic or polyurethane. Hang a real bell in the belfry.

Roof
(Cut 2)
(miter top edges to form a point)
(dotted line shows approximate roof overhang)

Middle Shelf Brace
(Cut 1)

Horizontal Shelves
(Cut 3)

Side Pieces
(Cut 2)
(miter top edges)

Decorative Shelf Brackets

These shelf brackets are designed to be used with shelving to create shelves that will suit individual needs. Cut as many brackets as needed and attach to wall. Shelving will rest on top of the brackets.

For all brackets 1 square = 1"

Bear Shelf Bracket
Great for baby's room.

Vine Covered Shelf Brackets
Cut out the center.

Country Sheep Shelf Brackets

Heart Shelf Brackets
Cut out around the heart.

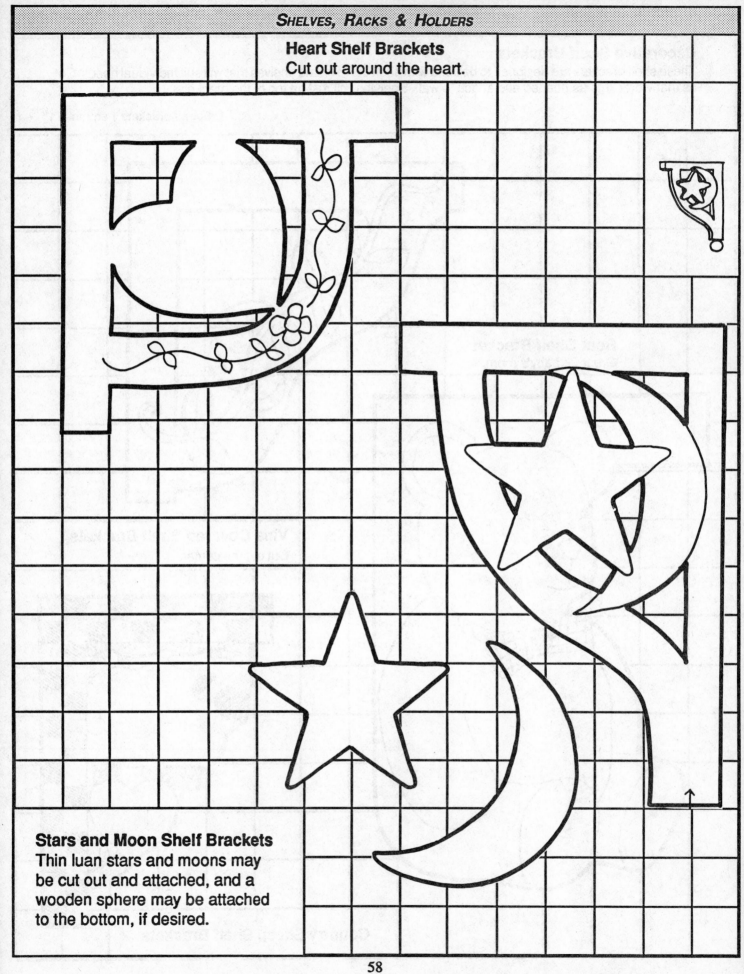

Stars and Moon Shelf Brackets
Thin luan stars and moons may
be cut out and attached, and a
wooden sphere may be attached
to the bottom, if desired.

Flag Magazine Rack

1 square = 1-1/2"

Cut 1 front, 1 back, 2 sides, and 1 bottom from 3/4" wood. Cut 1 star from 1/4" wood. Assemble using the diagram. Paint as indicated.

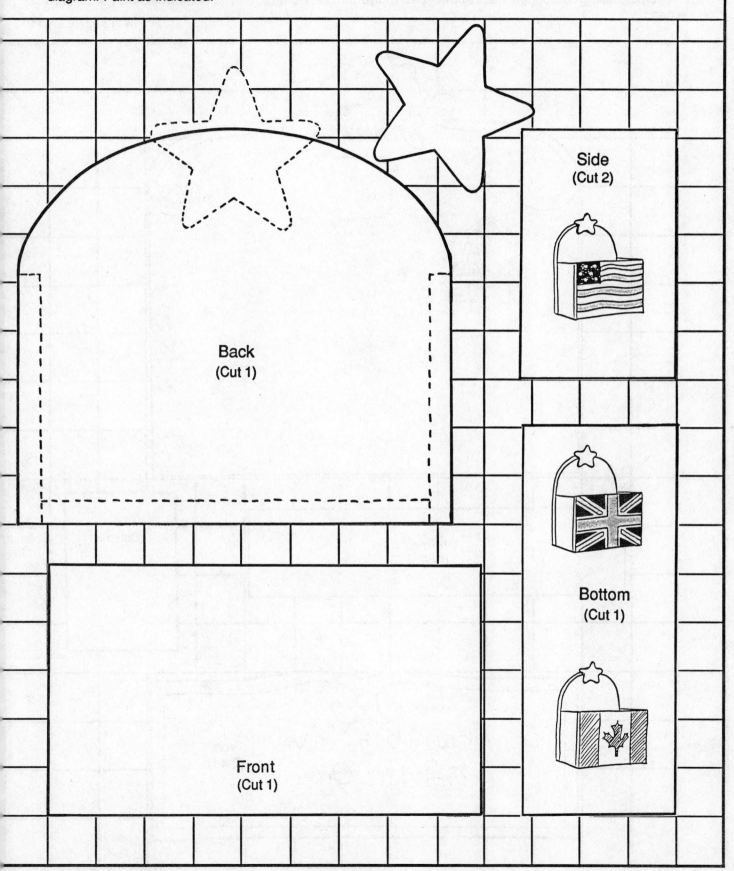

Back
(Cut 1)

Side
(Cut 2)

Bottom
(Cut 1)

Front
(Cut 1)

Garden Supply Holder

Cut 1 back, 2 sides, 1 front and 1 bottom from 3/4" wood. Drill holes in the side pieces as indicated by an X for shaker pegs. Assemble using the diagram. Paint and coat with polyurethane. Hang gloves, gardening hat, and gardening apron on the pegs.

1 square = 1-1/2"

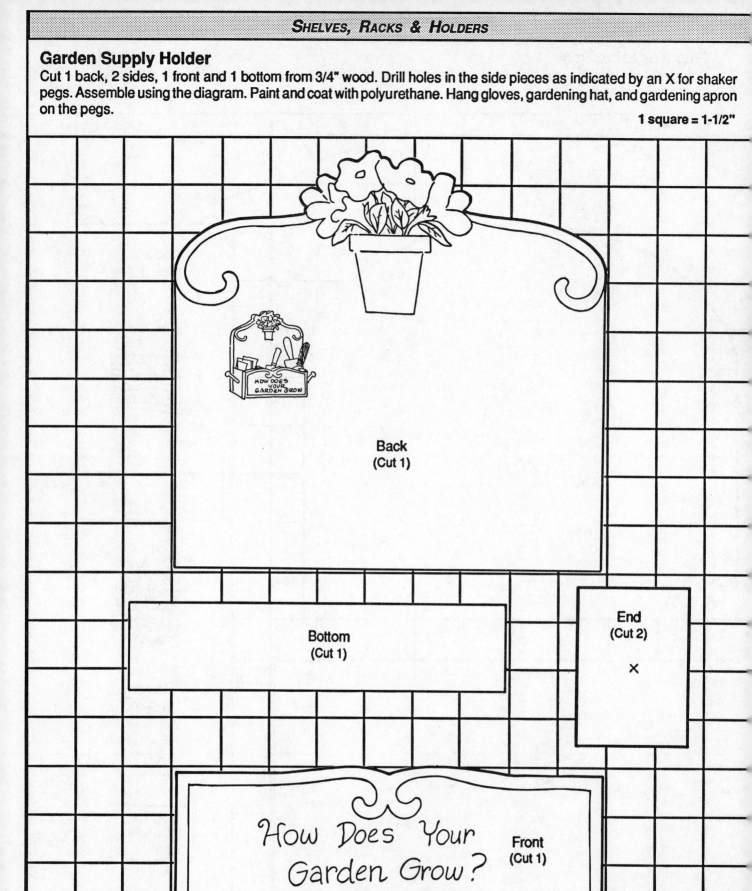

Back
(Cut 1)

Bottom
(Cut 1)

End
(Cut 2)

✕

How Does Your Garden Grow?

Front
(Cut 1)

Uncle Sam Dangling Shelf Sitter

1 square = 1/2"

Hungry Cat Dangling Shelf Sitter

1 square = 1/2"

1 square = 1/2"

Dangling Shelf Sitter Directions

Cut bodies from 1/2" to 3/4" wood. Cut arms and dangling objects from 1/4" wood. Drill holes in hands and dangling objects for string (see diagrams). Paint as indicated by the diagrams. Attach arms to bodies with wood glue. Attach dangling objects with string (as shown). When finished, each object will sit on the edge of a shelf and the dangling object will hang over the edge. These are ideal to decorate bookshelves because they take up so little shelf space.

Country Girl Dangling Shelf Sitter

Follow directions on previous page for Dangling Shelf Sitters. After finishing, glue excelsior or Spanish moss to head for hair.

1 square = 1/2"

Stretching Cat

Cut from 3/4" wood. This cat will sit up on it's hind legs. The front legs should rest on the wall. **Actual Size**

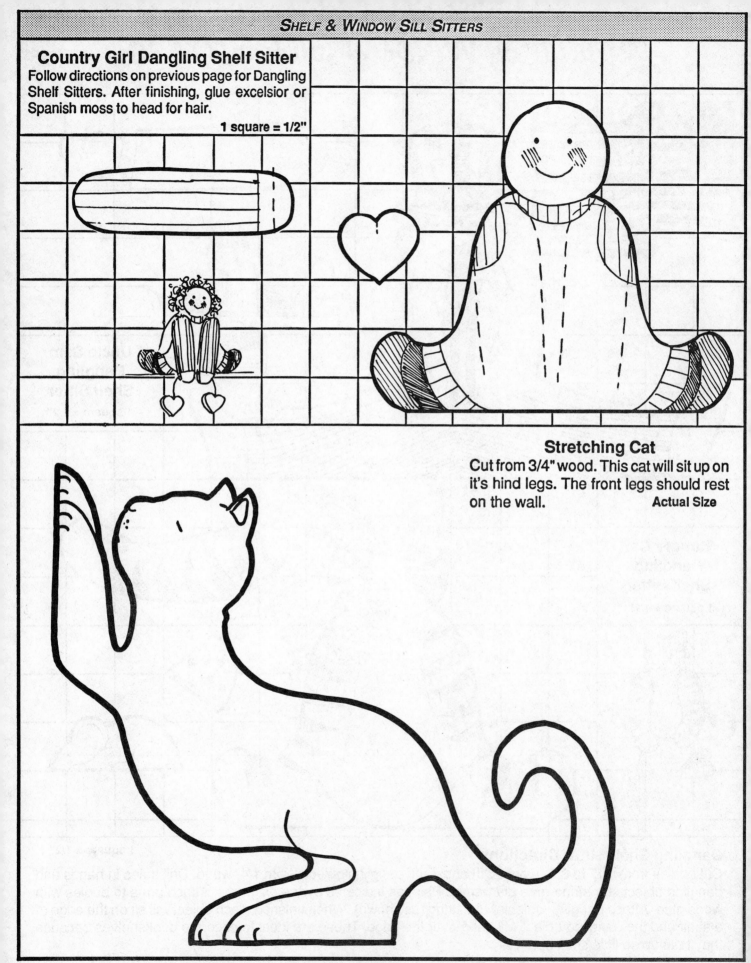

Occupational Window Sill Sitters
Actual Size

Construction Worker

Nurse

Babysitter

Secretary

Plumber

Postman

Sailor

Postal Service

63

Spider Plant

Fireman

Button Fern

Free-Standing Bushy Kitty

Cactus Flower

Toys & Games
Included are games and toys for all ages in a very interesting and useful variety. The toys and games may also be used for decorations. Just paint them in bright colors or to match your decor. Each pattern or pattern set will have its own individual directions.

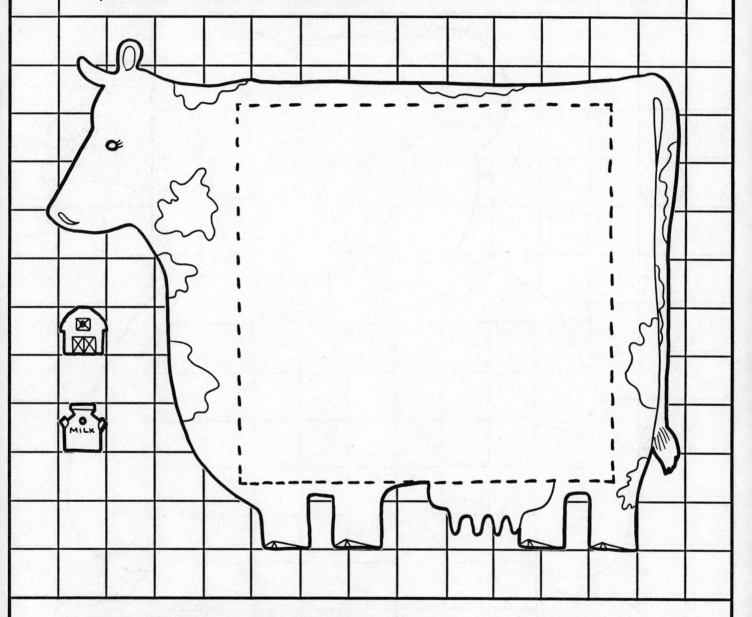

Spotted Cow Gameboard (for checkers or drafts)
Cut out 1 cow board, 12 milk can game pieces and 12 barn game pieces. A checkered grid should be placed on the cow and painted in alternating colors. A quick way to make a checkerboard design is to cut a stencil from cardboard or acetate, tape it in place, and, using stencil paint, stencil every other square. Be sure to alternate the squares on consecutive rows. Drill holes in each game piece to string onto jute to keep the game pieces together. Paint the cow black with white spots, the milk cans silver and black and the barn red. Paint the squares red. Coat with clear acrylic. String the playing pieces onto jute and tie around the cow's neck when not in use. Attach a hanger to the back if you want to hang the gameboard on the wall. Glue felt to the back to protect from damage to furniture.

1 square = 1"

Bear Gameboard Set (for checkers or drafts)

1 square = 1"

Cut out 1 bear board, 12 circle game pieces and 12 square game pieces. Paint to match your decor. A checkered grid should be placed on the bear and painted in alternating colors. A quick way to make a checkerboard design is to cut a stencil from cardboard or acetate, tape it in place, and, using stencil paint, stencil every other square. Be sure to alternate the squares on consecutive rows. Drill holes in the board where indicated by the X and also in each game piece to string a twine or ribbon to keep the game pieces together (see diagram). After painting all pieces, coat with clear acrylic. Attach a hanger to the back if you want to hang the gameboard on the wall. Glue felt to the back to protect from damage to furniture.

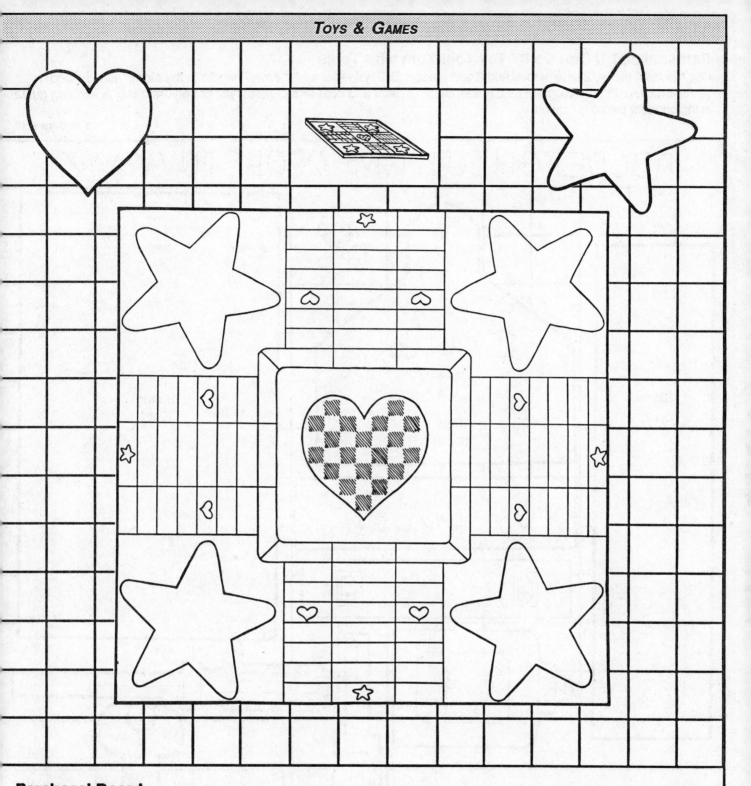

Parcheesi Board

Cut 1 board from 1/2" wood. Cut 4 large stars and 1 center heart from luan. Trace the entire board pattern onto the wooden board. Paint the center area behind the heart red. Paint the large heart with dark blue and taupe checks and glue to the center. The starting area for each player (behind the large stars) should have a dark blue background. Use country colors to paint the large luan star cutouts. We suggest country red, blue, green and gold. Glue the painted luan stars to each starting area (see diagram). Each center, homestretch area should be painted to correspond with a star. The outside areas where the playing pieces move around the board should be painted taupe. Use black-brown to paint all lines around each space section. All small stars should be painted yellow and all small hearts red. Optional: A trim may be added to form a ridge or tray.

1 square = 1-1/2"

Personalized "I Can Do It" Toy Tool Tote with Tools

Cut 1 bottom piece, 2 side pieces and 2 end pieces. Drill holes for a 5/8" dowel handle in the sides, as indicated by an X. Assemble using the diagram as a guide. Stain or paint and coat with clear acrylic or polyurethane. A lettering guide is included for personalization.

1 square = 1"

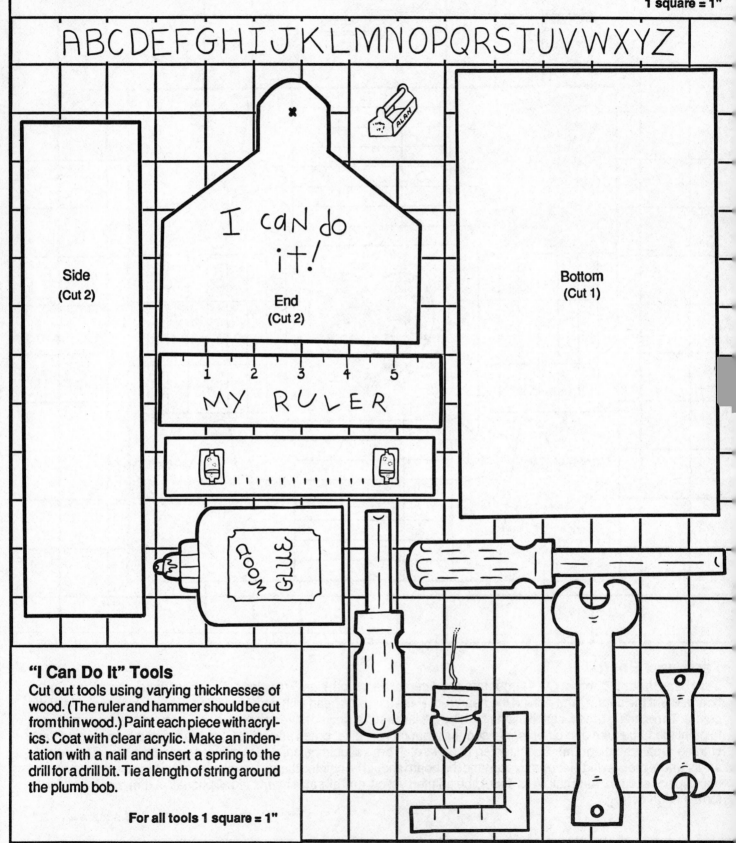

ABCDEFGHIJKLMNOPQRSTUVWXYZ

Side
(Cut 2)

I can do it!

End
(Cut 2)

MY RULER

1 2 3 4 5

Bottom
(Cut 1)

WOOD GLUE

"I Can Do It" Tools

Cut out tools using varying thicknesses of wood. (The ruler and hammer should be cut from thin wood.) Paint each piece with acrylics. Coat with clear acrylic. Make an indentation with a nail and insert a spring to the drill for a drill bit. Tie a length of string around the plumb bob.

For all tools 1 square = 1"

Wooden Airplane

Cut 1 fuselage, 1 wing, and 1 tail wing from 1/2" wood. Cut out the center of the fuselage for the wings (see pattern). Drill 3/4" hole above the wings for a 5/8" purchased figure. Cut 1 propeller from 1/8" wood. Assemble with wood glue and finishing nails, using the diagram. 1-1/4" wheels may be purchased and attached as shown. Paint or stain and coat with clear acrylic.

1 square = 1"

Use large blade for airplane propeller and helicopter rotary blade.

Wooden Helicopter

1 square = 1"

Cut 1 helicopter body from 1/2" wood. Drill 3/4" hole in the cockpit for a 5/8" purchased figure. Cut 1 large rotary blade and 2 small rotary blades from 1/8" wood. Assemble with wood glue and finishing nails, using the diagram. 1-1/4" wheels may be purchased and attached as shown. Paint or stain and coat with clear acrylic.

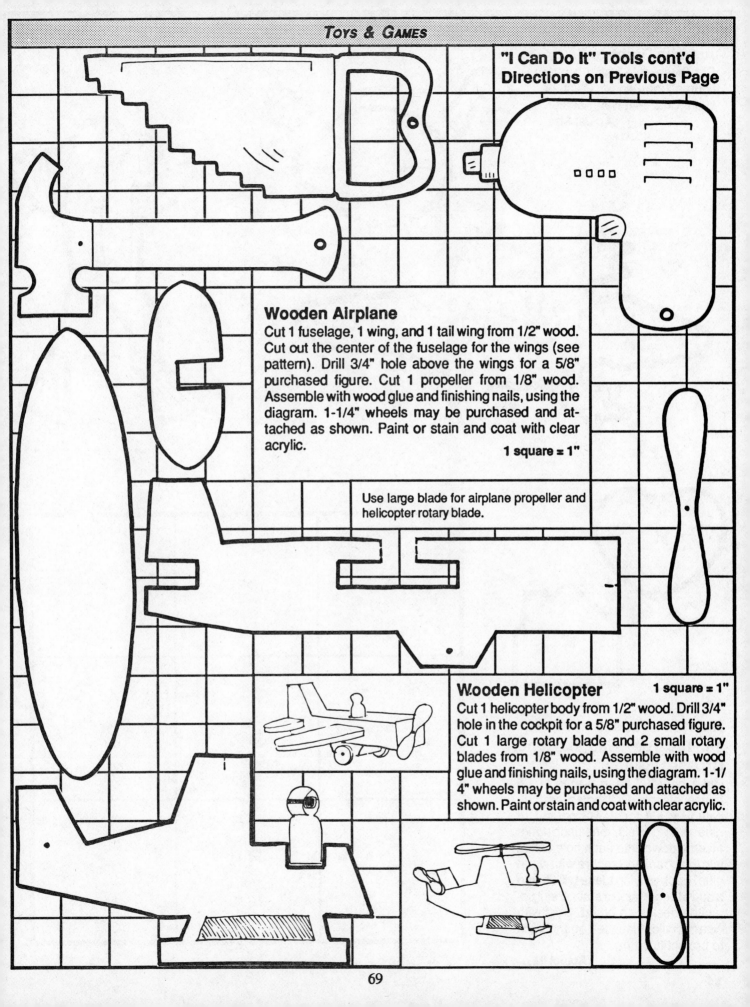

Aquatic Bathtub Toys

Cut these cute bathtub play figures from wood. Paint or stain. Coat with water sealer.
Actual Size

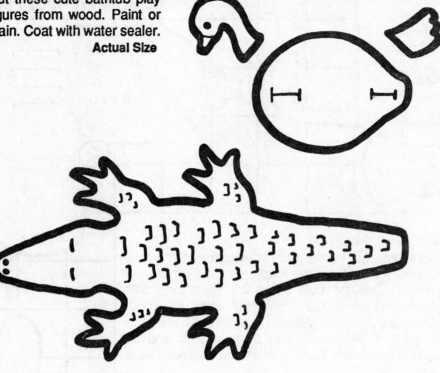

Hearts & Houses
Tic-Tac-Toe (Naughts and Crosses) Game

Cut 1 board, 5 heart pieces and 5 house pieces. Drill holes as indicated by X's for dowel pegs. Cut nine 3/8" dowels, one inch long. Insert a dowel into each hole drilled into the board and secure with wood glue. Each playing piece will fit onto a dowel peg. Paint or stain. Paint tic-tac-toe design on board. Coat with clear acrylic. Place felt on the back to protect furniture.

Actual Size

Cole Brothers Play Circus Set
The circus set includes a wagon with animals and circus figures that fit inside.

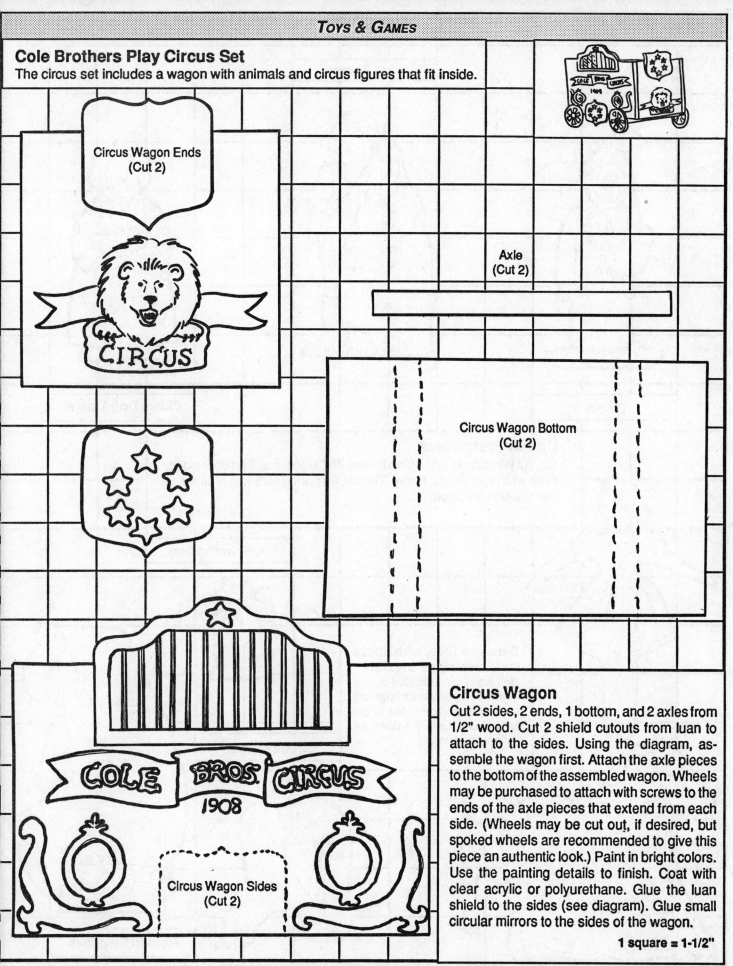

Circus Wagon Ends
(Cut 2)

Axle
(Cut 2)

Circus Wagon Bottom
(Cut 2)

CIRCUS

COLE BROS CIRCUS
1908

Circus Wagon Sides
(Cut 2)

Circus Wagon
Cut 2 sides, 2 ends, 1 bottom, and 2 axles from 1/2" wood. Cut 2 shield cutouts from luan to attach to the sides. Using the diagram, assemble the wagon first. Attach the axle pieces to the bottom of the assembled wagon. Wheels may be purchased to attach with screws to the ends of the axle pieces that extend from each side. (Wheels may be cut out, if desired, but spoked wheels are recommended to give this piece an authentic look.) Paint in bright colors. Use the painting details to finish. Coat with clear acrylic or polyurethane. Glue the luan shield to the sides (see diagram). Glue small circular mirrors to the sides of the wagon.

1 square = 1-1/2"

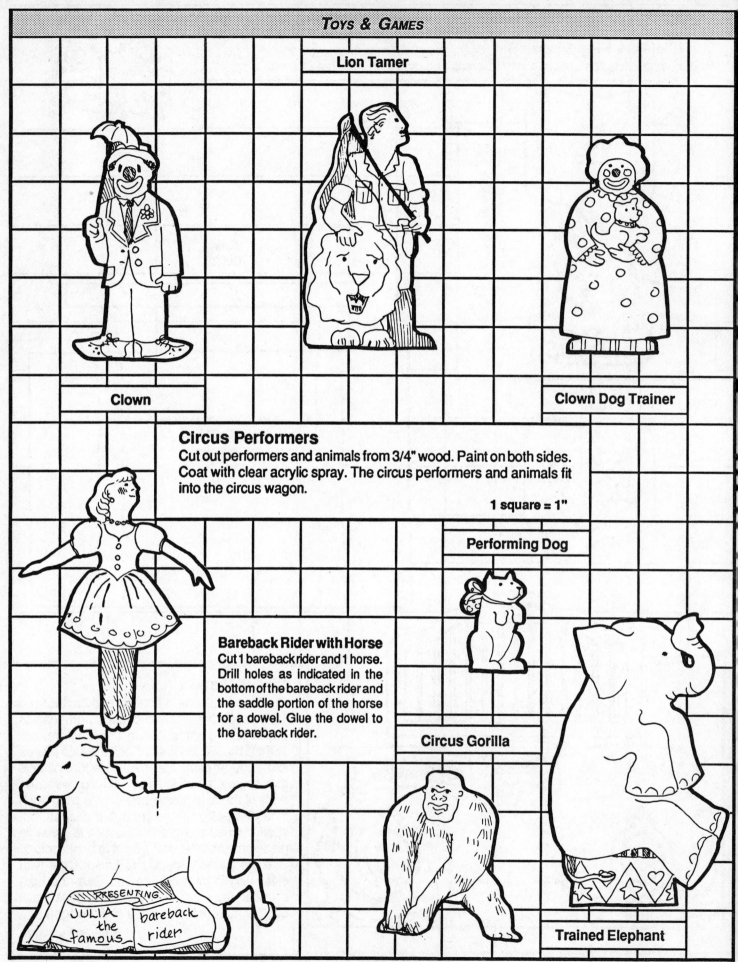

Lion Tamer

Clown

Clown Dog Trainer

Circus Performers

Cut out performers and animals from 3/4" wood. Paint on both sides. Coat with clear acrylic spray. The circus performers and animals fit into the circus wagon.

1 square = 1"

Performing Dog

Bareback Rider with Horse

Cut 1 bareback rider and 1 horse. Drill holes as indicated in the bottom of the bareback rider and the saddle portion of the horse for a dowel. Glue the dowel to the bareback rider.

Circus Gorilla

PRESENTING
JULIA
the
famous
bareback
rider

Trained Elephant

Barn Bottom
(Cut 1)

Barn Front/Back
(Cut 2)

Top Brace
(Cut 2)

Side Brace
(Cut 2)

Barn Front Roof
(Cut 1)

Americana Barn Play Set

Cut 2 side pieces, 2 front/back pieces, 1 bottom piece, 1 front roof piece, 1 back roof piece, 2 top braces and 2 side braces from 1/2" wood. Cut windows out on side pieces. Assemble the pieces, using the diagram. The back roof piece will be attached to the barn but the front roof piece will sit on top of the roof and will be lifted off so that the animals will fit inside. Paint as indicated. Coat with clear acrylic or polyurethane.   **1 square = 1-1/2"**

Barn Sides
(Cut 2)

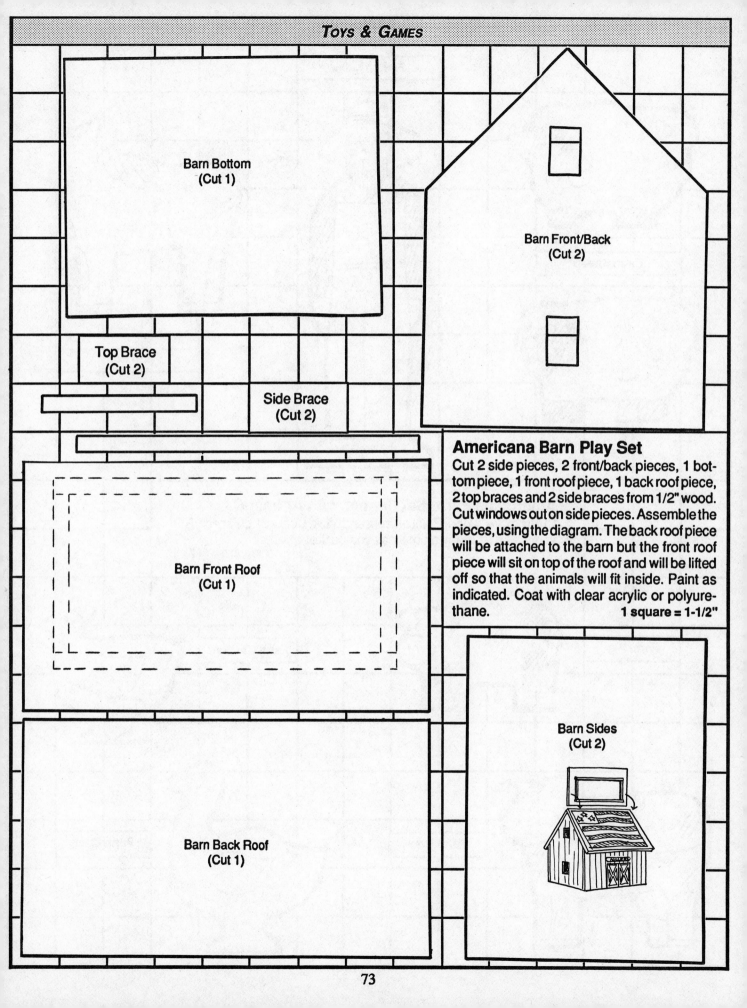

Barn Back Roof
(Cut 1)

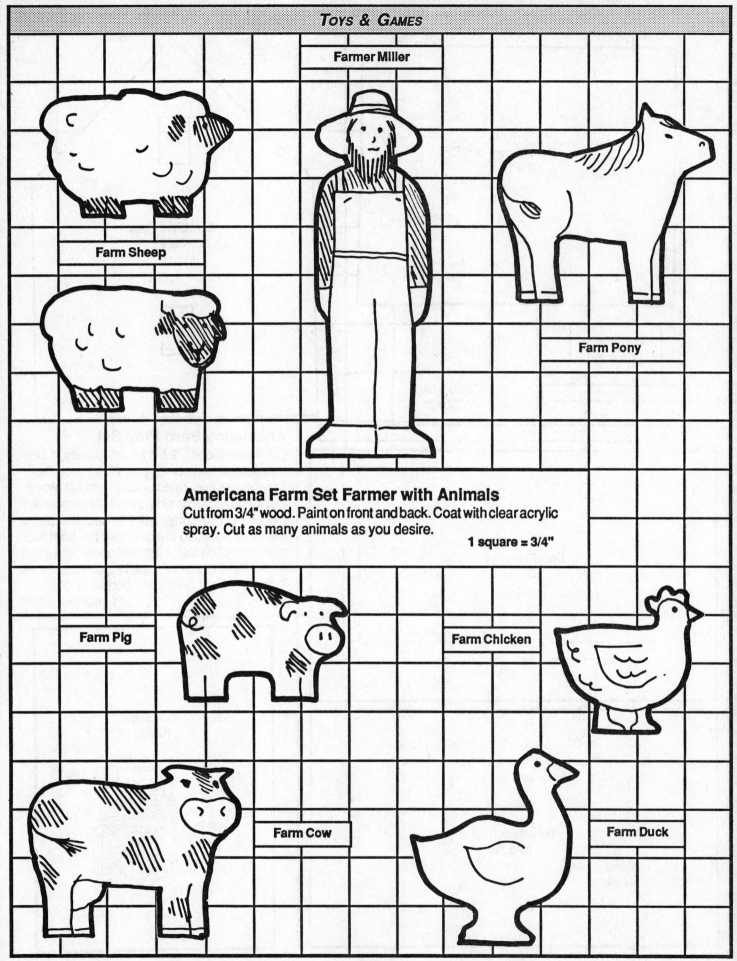

Farmer Miller

Farm Sheep

Farm Pony

Americana Farm Set Farmer with Animals
Cut from 3/4" wood. Paint on front and back. Coat with clear acrylic spray. Cut as many animals as you desire.

1 square = 3/4"

Farm Pig

Farm Chicken

Farm Cow

Farm Duck

74

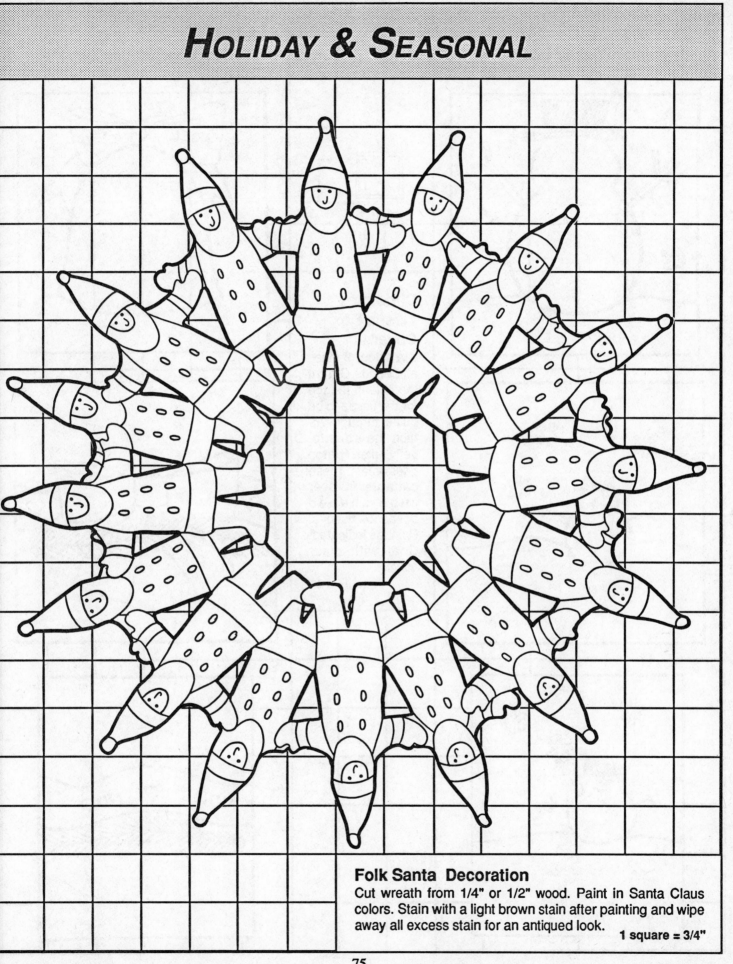

Folk Santa Decoration

Cut wreath from 1/4" or 1/2" wood. Paint in Santa Claus colors. Stain with a light brown stain after painting and wipe away all excess stain for an antiqued look.

1 square = 3/4"

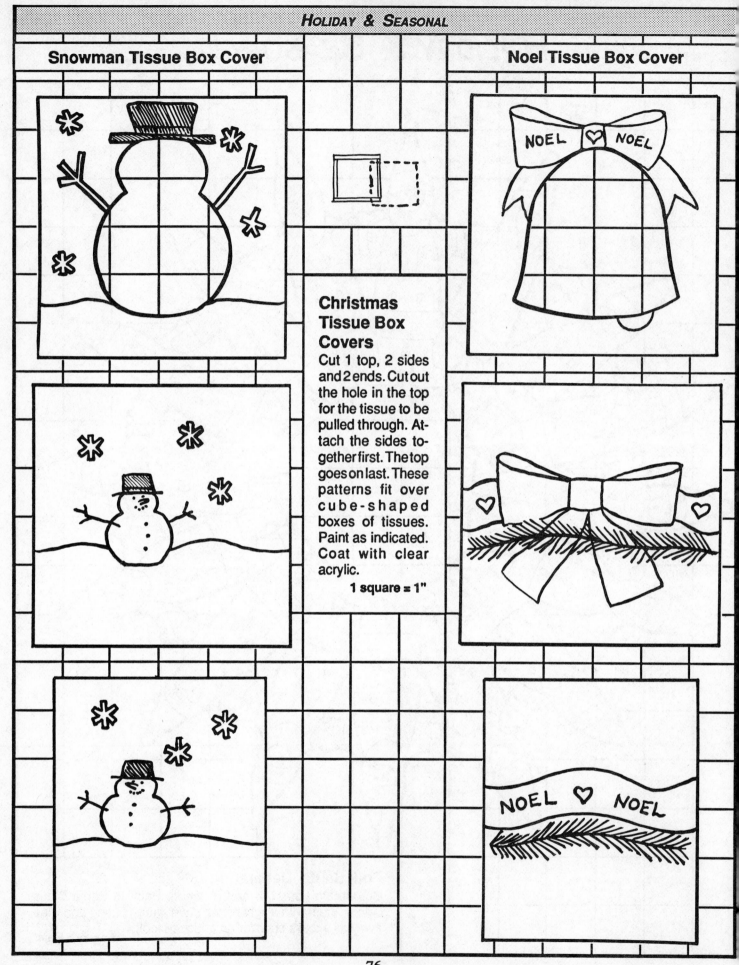

Snowman Tissue Box Cover

Noel Tissue Box Cover

Christmas Tissue Box Covers

Cut 1 top, 2 sides and 2 ends. Cut out the hole in the top for the tissue to be pulled through. Attach the sides together first. The top goes on last. These patterns fit over cube-shaped boxes of tissues. Paint as indicated. Coat with clear acrylic.

1 square = 1"

NOEL ♡ NOEL

NOEL ♡ NOEL

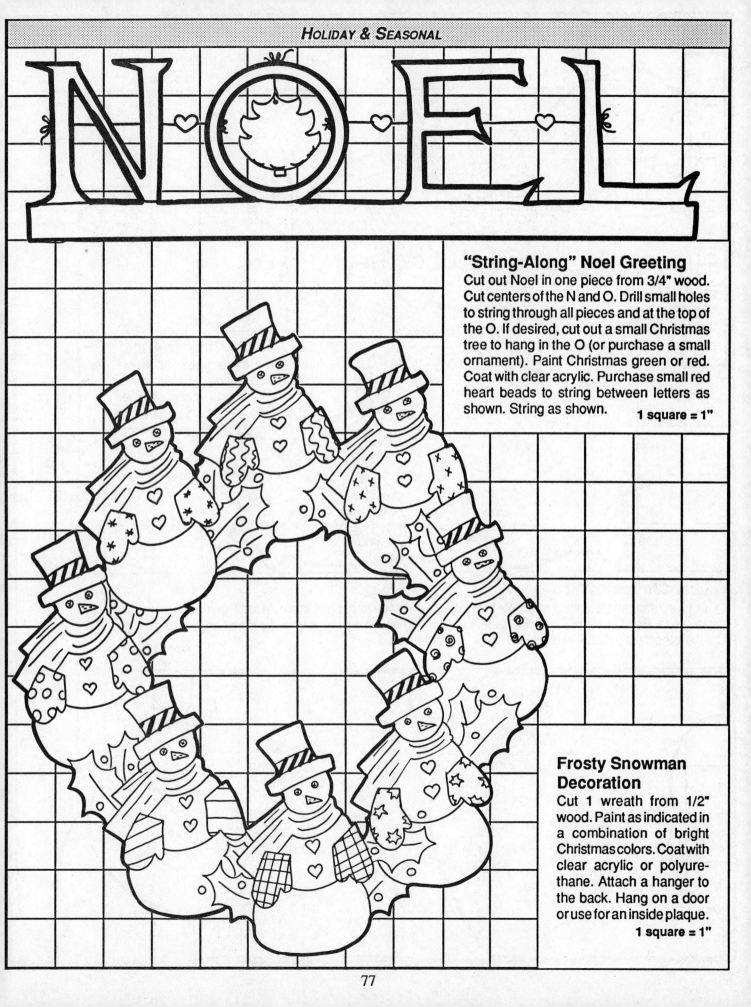

"String-Along" Noel Greeting

Cut out Noel in one piece from 3/4" wood. Cut centers of the N and O. Drill small holes to string through all pieces and at the top of the O. If desired, cut out a small Christmas tree to hang in the O (or purchase a small ornament). Paint Christmas green or red. Coat with clear acrylic. Purchase small red heart beads to string between letters as shown. String as shown.

1 square = 1"

Frosty Snowman Decoration

Cut 1 wreath from 1/2" wood. Paint as indicated in a combination of bright Christmas colors. Coat with clear acrylic or polyurethane. Attach a hanger to the back. Hang on a door or use for an inside plaque.

1 square = 1"

Mexican Christmas Plaque

1 square = 1"

¡Feliz Navidad!

Alleluia Chorus Angel

Cut 1 angel from 1/2" wood. Finish as indicated. Hang over a doorway or window frame.

1 square = 1"

ALLELUIA

Merry Christmas Sled

Cut 1 sled seat and 2 skids. Drill a hole in the skids for a rope to hang. Assemble sled, using the diagram as a guide. Paint or stain. Coat with clear acrylic. Hang on the wall or door using rope tied from one skid to the other. Optional: Attach holly or greenery to the sled.

1 square = 1"

Merry Christmas!

CELEBRATE Jesus!

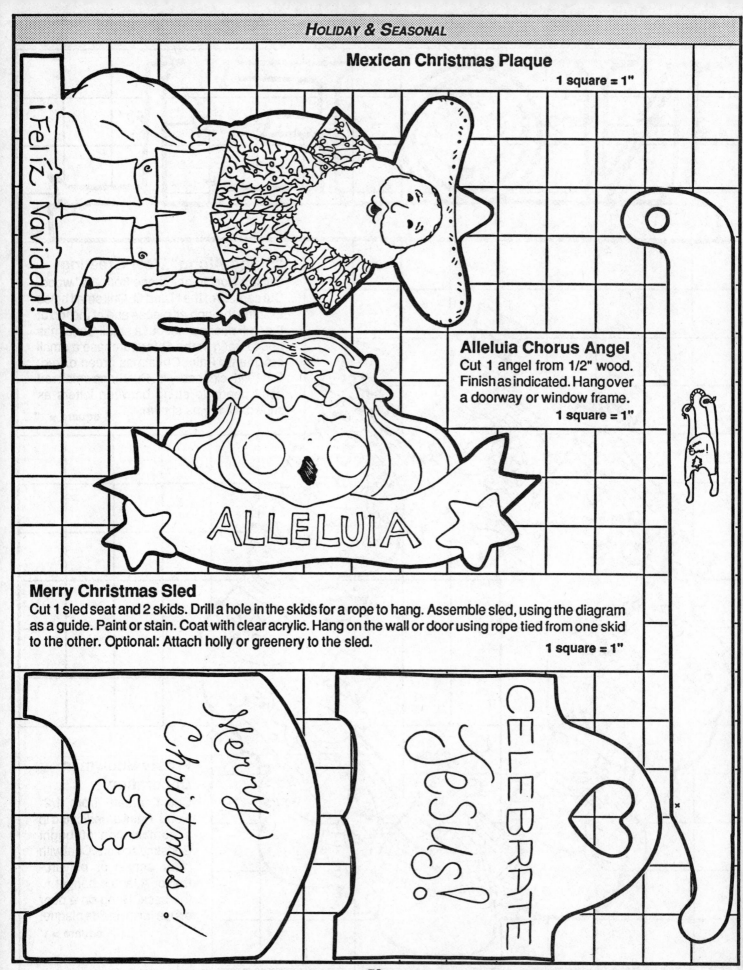

Intricate Snowflake

Cut 1 snowflake from thin wood. There are many inside cuts so care will need to be taken to prevent the wood from splitting.

Actual Size

Christmas Candy Cane Holder

Cut 1 bed headboard, 1 bed footboard from 3/4" wood. Cut one 5" x 3" x 2-1/2" piece to go in between the headboard and the footboard. Drill holes for the candy canes as shown. Glue all sections together. Glue batting on top of the middle section and cover it entirely with fabric (see diagram).

1 square = 3/4"

Chunky Angel   1 square = 1"

Cut 1 angel from 1-1/2" wood. Paint front and back. Glue excelsior, angel hair or dried Spanish moss for hair.

BEARY-MERRY CHRISTMAS

Beary Merry Christmas Triple Switchplate Cover

Cut 1 switchplate cover back and 1 bear from thin wood. Cut out holes for switches (don't forget to cut a hole through the bear). Drill holes for screws. Paint as indicated and glue together. Adjust the size of switchplate for single and double plates.

**Season's Greetings
Welcome Sign**   1 square = 1"

SEASON'S GREETINGS!

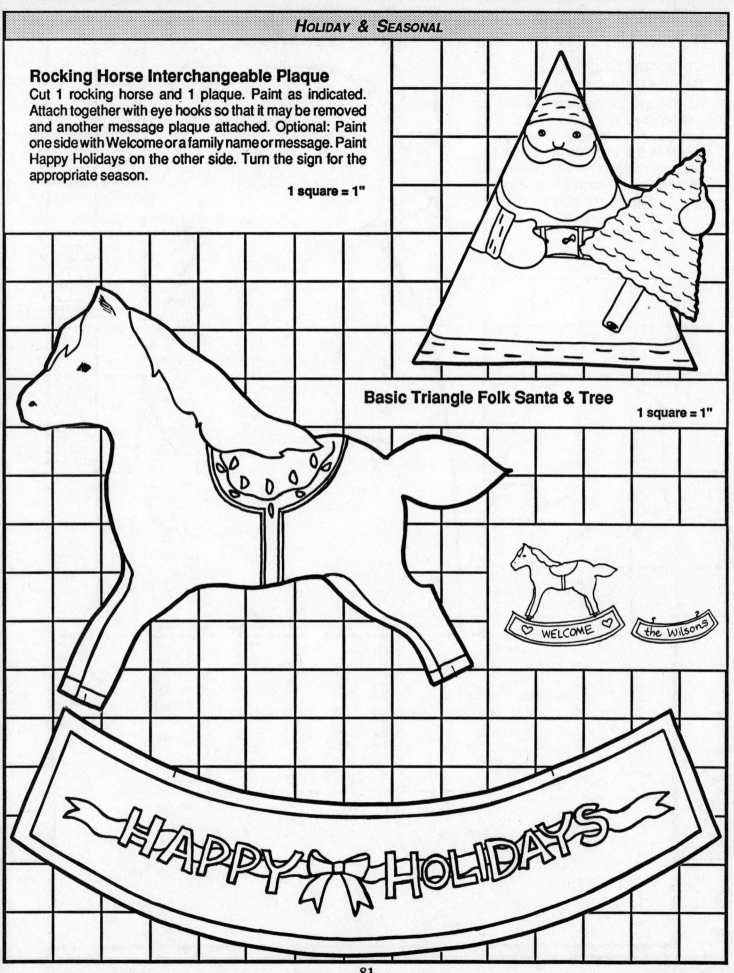

Rocking Horse Interchangeable Plaque

Cut 1 rocking horse and 1 plaque. Paint as indicated. Attach together with eye hooks so that it may be removed and another message plaque attached. Optional: Paint one side with Welcome or a family name or message. Paint Happy Holidays on the other side. Turn the sign for the appropriate season.

1 square = 1"

Basic Triangle Folk Santa & Tree

1 square = 1"

WELCOME

the Wilsons

HAPPY HOLIDAYS

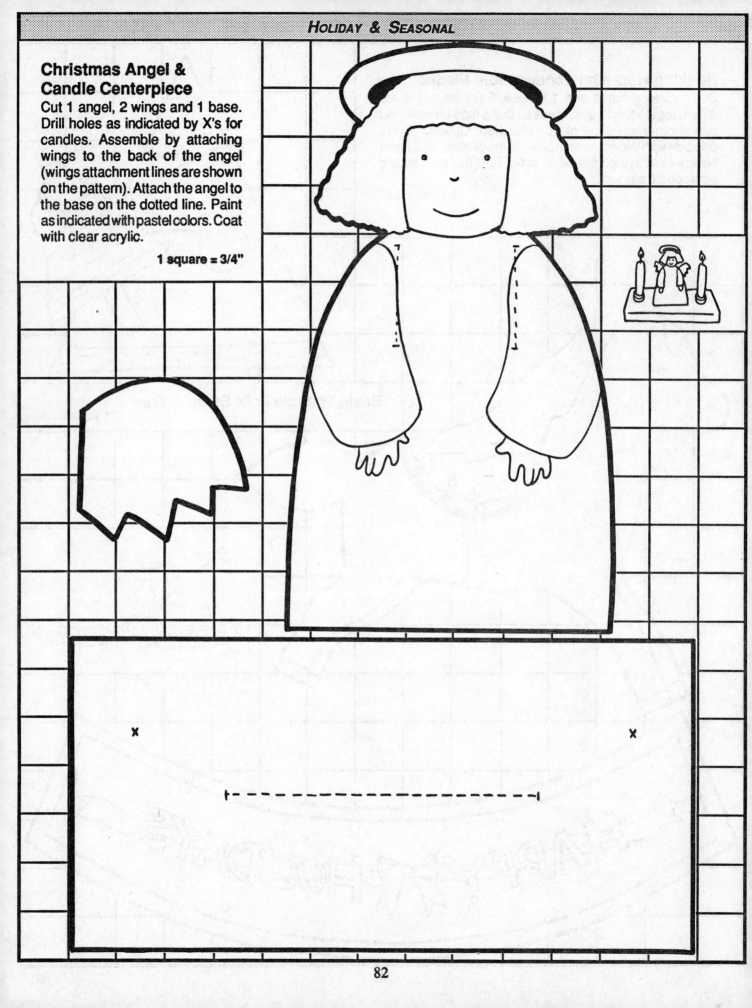

Christmas Angel & Candle Centerpiece

Cut 1 angel, 2 wings and 1 base. Drill holes as indicated by X's for candles. Assemble by attaching wings to the back of the angel (wings attachment lines are shown on the pattern). Attach the angel to the base on the dotted line. Paint as indicated with pastel colors. Coat with clear acrylic.

1 square = 3/4"

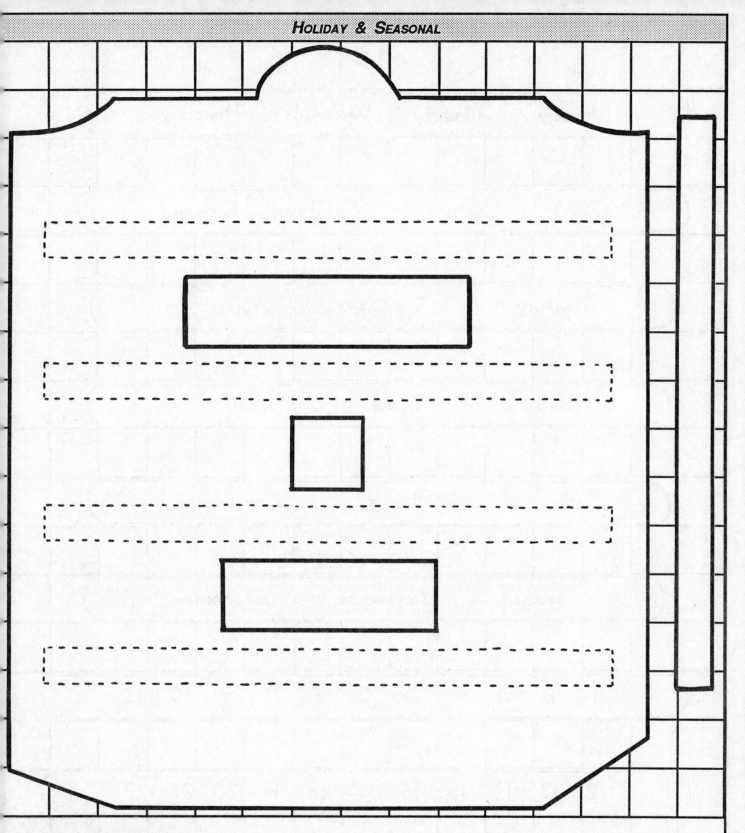

Perpetual Strip Calendar

Cut 2 front/back pieces. Cut 4 tracking strips from 1/2" wood. Cut calendar strips from 1/4" wood. Both sides of the strips may be used to paint names and numbers, if desired. Cut the windows out of the front piece. The back piece will not have windows. The strips will slide through and the dates will show through the windows. To assemble, attach the strips between the front and back layers in the spaces marked by dotted lines. Stain the front and back pieces. Paint the strips a color that is easy to read. Paint on all days and dates.

1 square = 3/4"

Monday   Tuesday   Wednesday   Thursday

Friday   Saturday   Sunday   Fun-day

JANUARY   FEBRUARY   MARCH

APRIL   MAY   JUNE

JULY   AUGUST   SEPTEMBER

OCTOBER   NOVEMBER   DECEMBER

1   2   3   4   5   6   7   8   9   10   11

12   13   14   15   16   17   18   19   20   21   22

23   24   25   26   27   28   29   30   31   ?

Calendar Strips for Perpetual Calendar
See directions on previous page

1 square = 1-1/2"

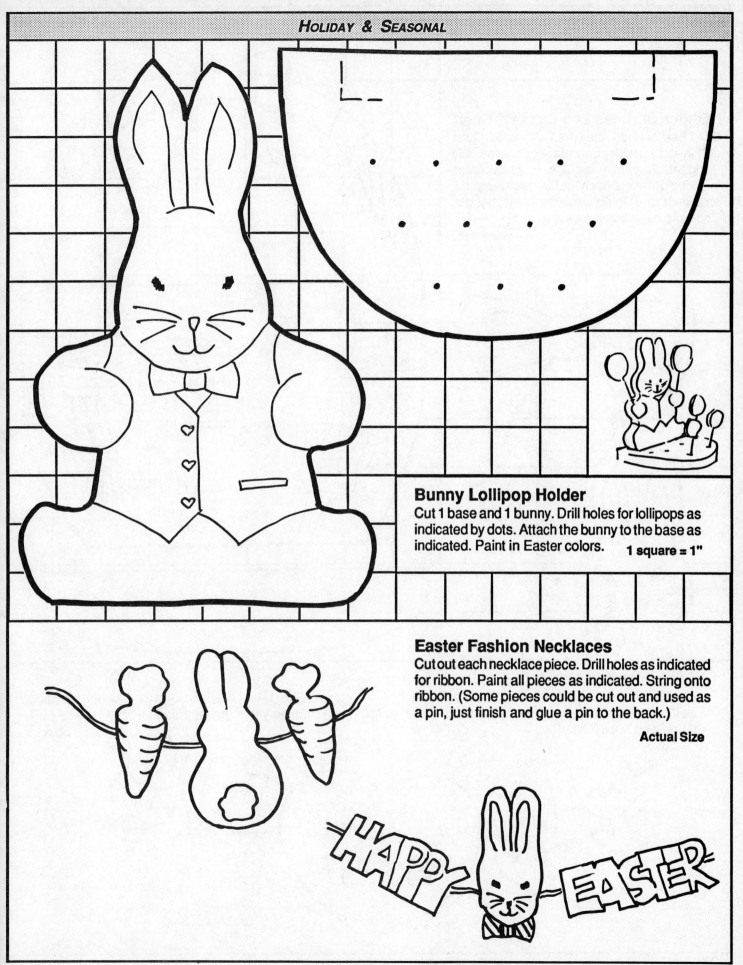

Bunny Lollipop Holder
Cut 1 base and 1 bunny. Drill holes for lollipops as indicated by dots. Attach the bunny to the base as indicated. Paint in Easter colors. **1 square = 1"**

Easter Fashion Necklaces
Cut out each necklace piece. Drill holes as indicated for ribbon. Paint all pieces as indicated. String onto ribbon. (Some pieces could be cut out and used as a pin, just finish and glue a pin to the back.)

Actual Size

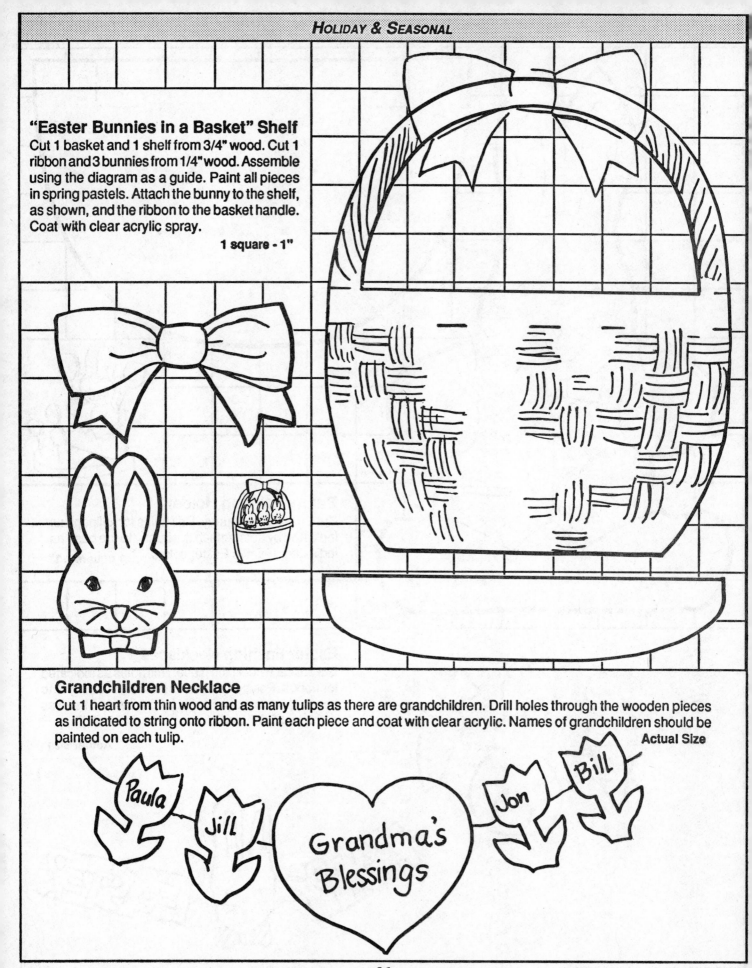

"Easter Bunnies in a Basket" Shelf

Cut 1 basket and 1 shelf from 3/4" wood. Cut 1 ribbon and 3 bunnies from 1/4" wood. Assemble using the diagram as a guide. Paint all pieces in spring pastels. Attach the bunny to the shelf, as shown, and the ribbon to the basket handle. Coat with clear acrylic spray.

1 square - 1"

Grandchildren Necklace

Cut 1 heart from thin wood and as many tulips as there are grandchildren. Drill holes through the wooden pieces as indicated to string onto ribbon. Paint each piece and coat with clear acrylic. Names of grandchildren should be painted on each tulip.

Actual Size

Paula Jill Grandma's Blessings Jon Bill

All Occasion Pie and Cake Toppers

Cut from thin wood or luan. Hot glue to a short length of 1/4" dowel. Use to quickly decorate for any occasion. Paint on your own message, if desired.

Actual Size

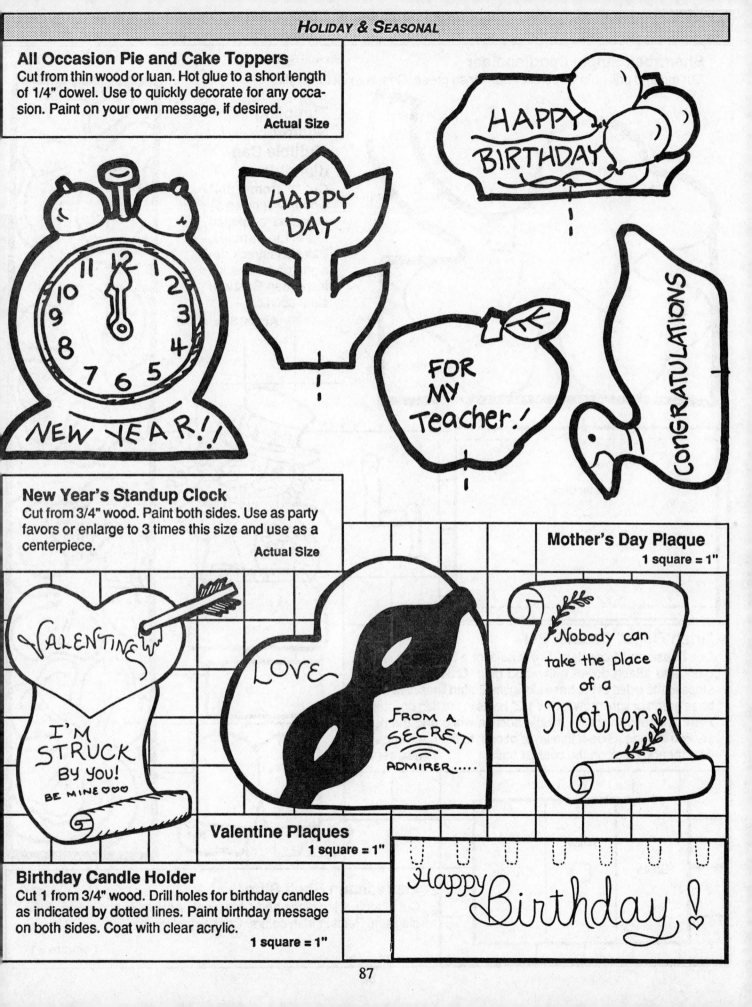

HAPPY BIRTHDAY

HAPPY DAY

FOR MY Teacher.!

CONGRATULATIONS

NEW YEAR!!

New Year's Standup Clock

Cut from 3/4" wood. Paint both sides. Use as party favors or enlarge to 3 times this size and use as a centerpiece.

Actual Size

Mother's Day Plaque
1 square = 1"

VALENTINE
I'M STRUCK BY YOU!
BE MINE♡♡♡

LOVE
FROM A SECRET ADMIRER.....

Nobody can take the place of a Mother

Valentine Plaques
1 square = 1"

Birthday Candle Holder

Cut 1 from 3/4" wood. Drill holes for birthday candles as indicated by dotted lines. Paint birthday message on both sides. Coat with clear acrylic.

1 square = 1"

Happy Birthday!

87

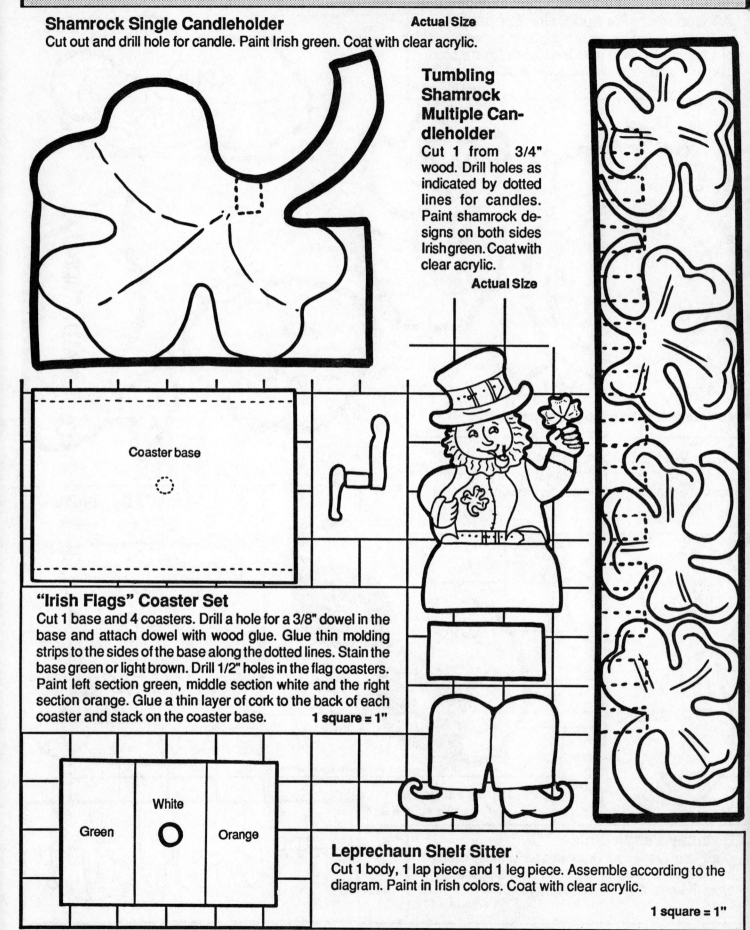

Shamrock Single Candleholder

Cut out and drill hole for candle. Paint Irish green. Coat with clear acrylic.

Actual Size

Tumbling Shamrock Multiple Candleholder

Cut 1 from 3/4" wood. Drill holes as indicated by dotted lines for candles. Paint shamrock designs on both sides Irish green. Coat with clear acrylic.

Actual Size

Coaster base

"Irish Flags" Coaster Set

Cut 1 base and 4 coasters. Drill a hole for a 3/8" dowel in the base and attach dowel with wood glue. Glue thin molding strips to the sides of the base along the dotted lines. Stain the base green or light brown. Drill 1/2" holes in the flag coasters. Paint left section green, middle section white and the right section orange. Glue a thin layer of cork to the back of each coaster and stack on the coaster base. **1 square = 1"**

Green White Orange

Leprechaun Shelf Sitter

Cut 1 body, 1 lap piece and 1 leg piece. Assemble according to the diagram. Paint in Irish colors. Coat with clear acrylic.

1 square = 1"

Fruit Basket Doorstop
Cut 1 fruit basket and 1 base. Attach together at the dotted line. Paint as indicated and coat with acrylic spray or polyurethane.

1 square = 1"

Cat and Mouse Doorstop

Cut 1 cat, 1 mouse and 1 base. Attach mouse and cat to base as indicated by dotted lines. Fasten from underneath with wood screws. Paint cat a tabby color and the mouse gray or brown. Stain the base and coat with clear acrylic or polyurethane.

1 square = 1"

American Southwestern Adobe Doorstop

Cut 1 adobe house and 1 base. Attach together at the dotted line. Paint as indicated and coat with acrylic spray or polyurethane.

1 square = 3/4"

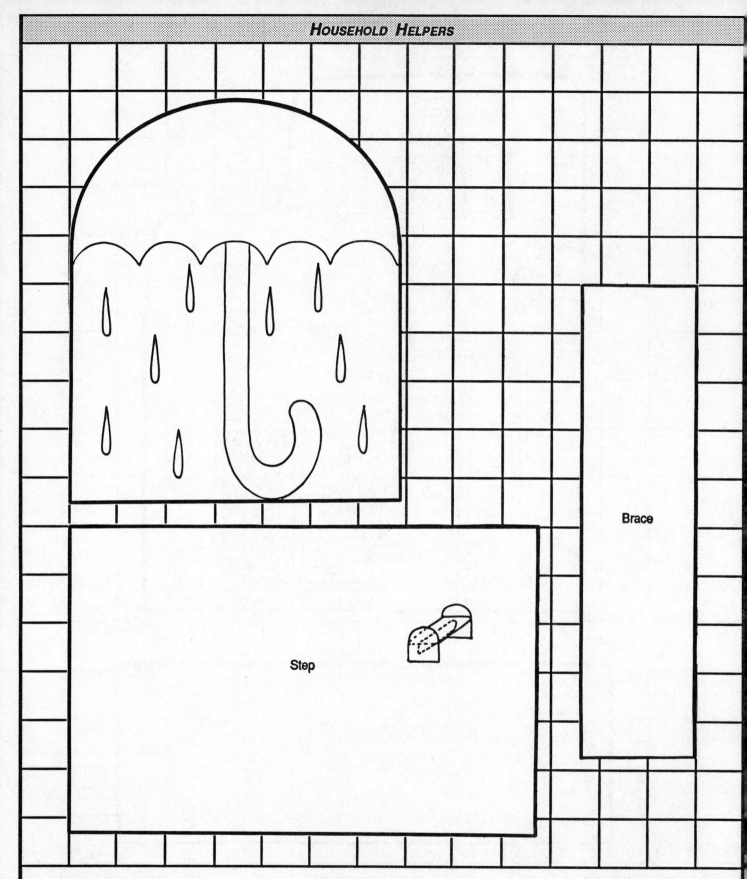

Brace

Step

Rainy Day Stool

Cut 2 sides and 1 step. Cut a 1 x 2 for a brace, the same length as the step. Assemble the stool as indicated by the diagram. Attach the brace for support. Paint and coat with clear acrylic.

1 square = 1"

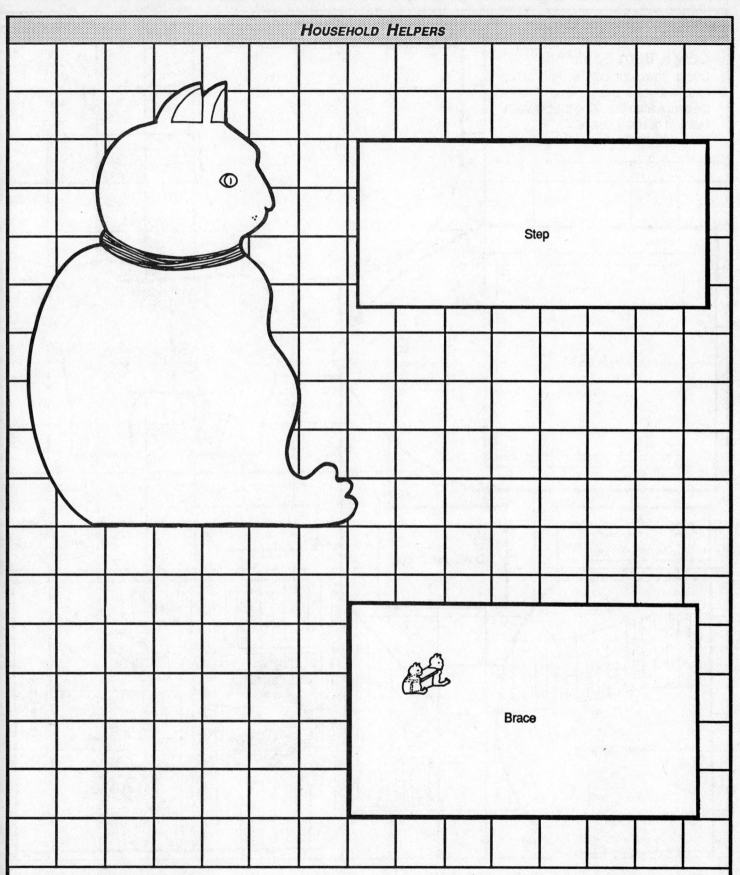

Step

Brace

Kitty One-Step Stool
Cut 2 sides, 1 support brace and 1 step. Attach sides to brace. (The brace will be flush with the floor on the bottom and will support the step on the top.) Paint as indicated and coat with clear acrylic.

1 square = 1-1/2"

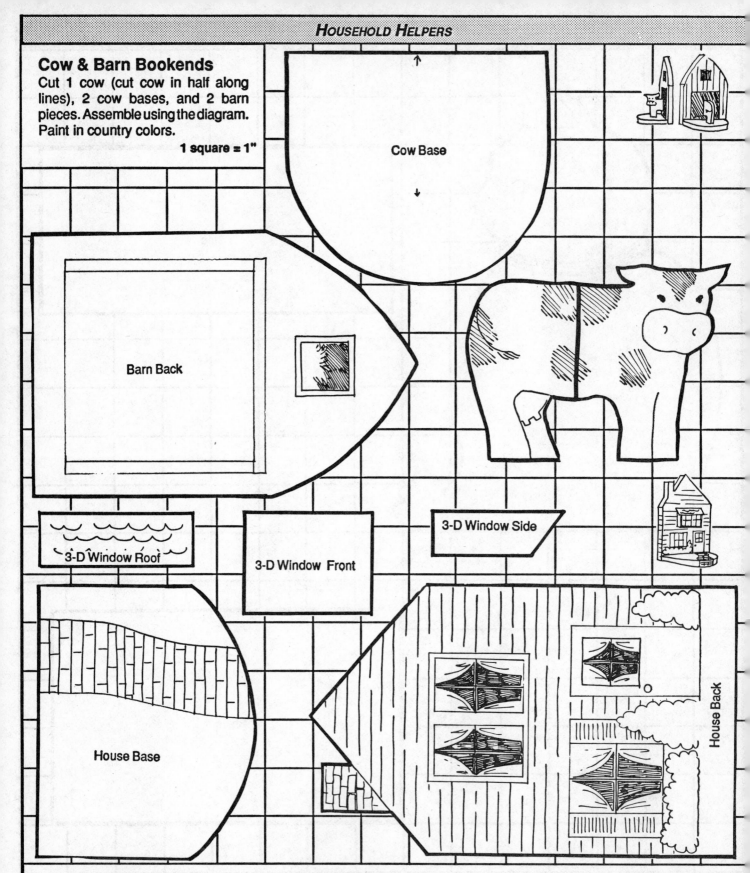

Cow & Barn Bookends

Cut 1 cow (cut cow in half along lines), 2 cow bases, and 2 barn pieces. Assemble using the diagram. Paint in country colors.

1 square = 1"

Cow Base

Barn Back

3-D Window Roof

3-D Window Front

3-D Window Side

House Base

House Back

House Bookends with Optional 3-D Windows

Cut 2 house pieces and 2 bases. If desired, a bay window may be glued to the front for a 3-D effect. For the window, cut 2 sides, 1 front and 1 roof from 1/8" wood. Assemble with hot glue and glue to the house window space. Assemble the bookends using the diagram. Paint and coat with clear acrylic.

1 square = 1"

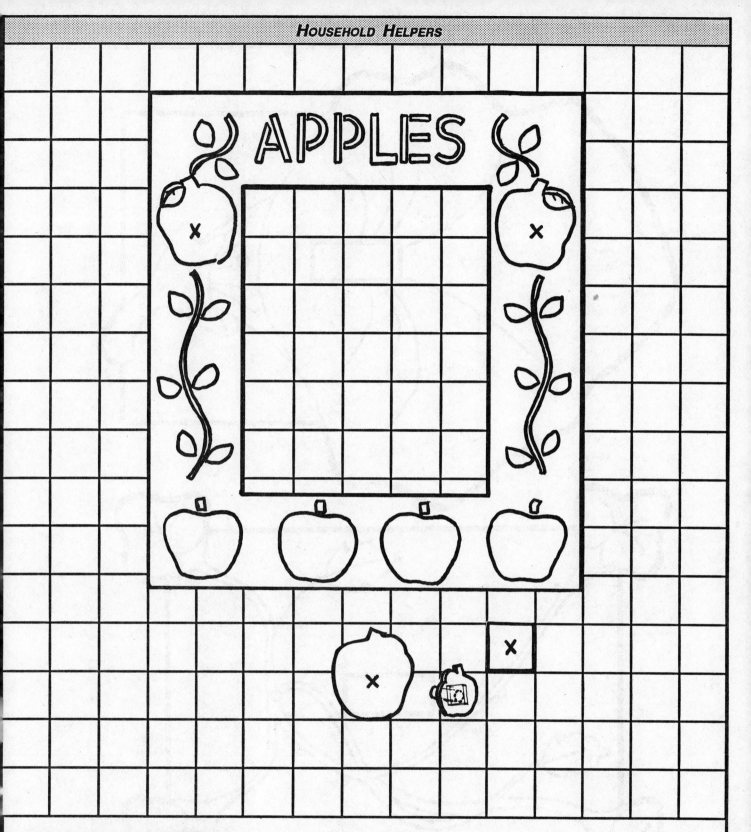

Country Apples Hall Mirror

Cut 1 mirror base from 1/2" wood. Finish the base with apple designs. If desired, cut out apples from thin wood to attach to frame base. Drill holes for shaker pegs on each side of the mirror frame. Attach a mirror to the center. Dowel pegs may be cut out to hang alongside the mirror. Cut apples from 1/2" wood. Cut a square from 3/4" wood to attach to the center of the apple. Drill a hole in the center for pegs. Attach pegs with wood glue. (See diagram for assembly of apple pegs.)

1 square = 1-1/2"

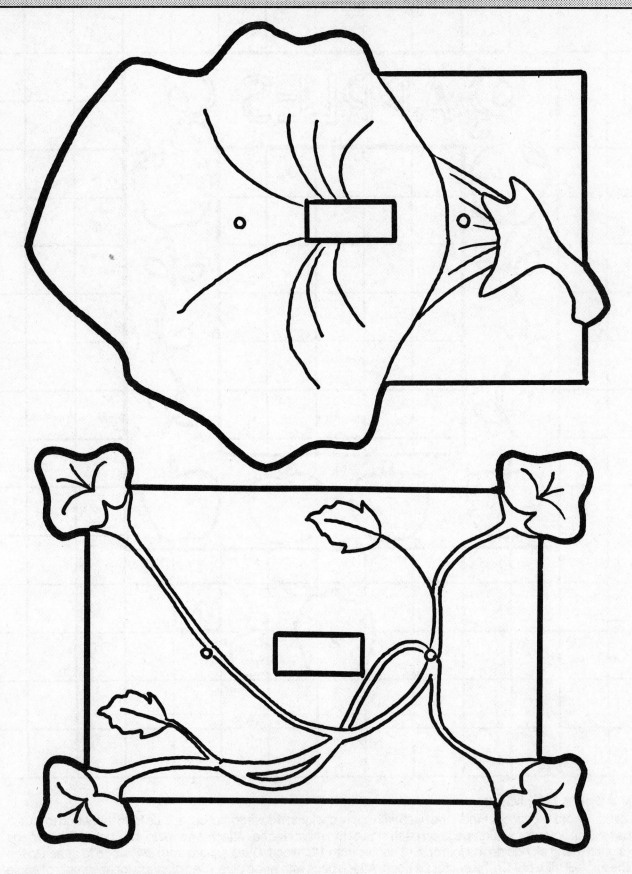

Custom-Cut Switchplates
Cut plates from thin wood or luan. Cut holes for light switches. Drill holes for screws. Paint to match decor.

Actual Size

Personalized Refrigerator Magnet Frame

Cut 1 frame from thin, light wood. Paint as indicated. Coat with clear acrylic spray. Attach magnet strips to the frame back close to the inner edge to hold paper properly. Use to display children's artwork.

1 square = 1"

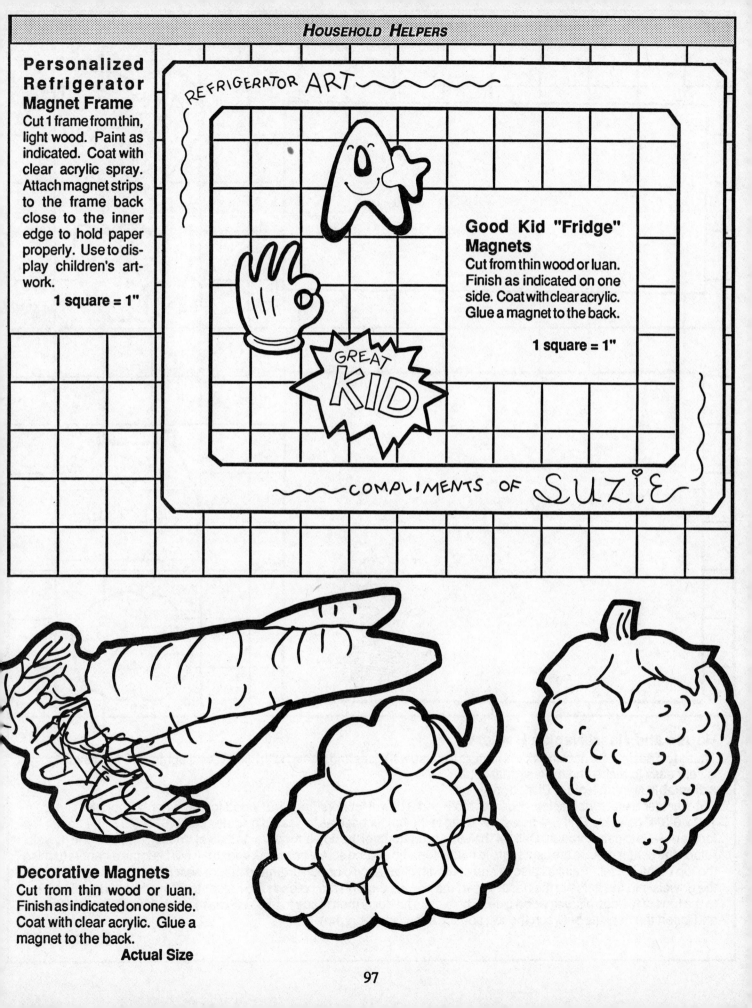

REFRIGERATOR ART

A+

GREAT KID

COMPLIMENTS OF SUZIE

Good Kid "Fridge" Magnets

Cut from thin wood or luan. Finish as indicated on one side. Coat with clear acrylic. Glue a magnet to the back.

1 square = 1"

Decorative Magnets

Cut from thin wood or luan. Finish as indicated on one side. Coat with clear acrylic. Glue a magnet to the back.

Actual Size

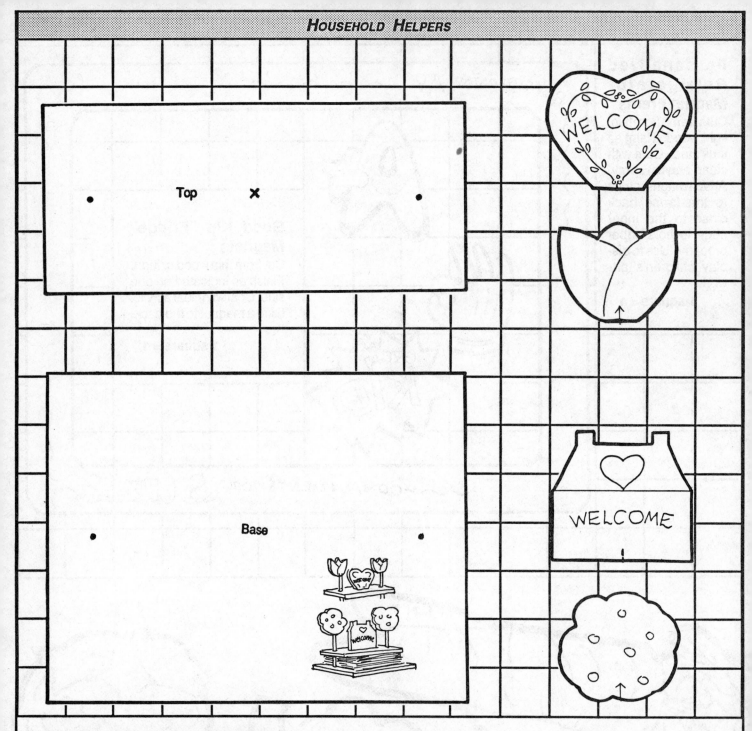

House and Heart Napkin Holders

These two designs for napkin holders feature a house with trees and a heart with tulips (see diagrams). This clever design is very easy to make and makes great gifts.

Adjustable Napkin Holder Directions

Cut 1 holder base, 1 holder top, 1 center motif and 2 dowel toppers from 1/2" wood for each napkin holder. Cut 2 1/4" x 6-3/4" dowels . Drill 1/4" holes 1/2" deep in the holder base as indicated by dots. Drill 3/8" holes in the holder top for the dowels to pass through. Drill 1/4" holes in the bottoms of the dowel toppers, 1/2" deep to insert the top of the dowels. Attach the center motif to the center of the holder top with a wood screw from underneath. It will become a handle to raise the top of the holder. Paint all pieces and coat with clear acrylic or polyurethane before assembly. To assemble, glue the dowels into the holes in the base. Insert the dowels through the holes in the holder top. Attach the dowel toppers to the tops of the dowels with wood glue. The napkin holder is then ready to use. Lift the top with the center motif handle and insert the napkins between the top and the base (see diagram).

1 square = 1"

Cactus & Adobe Bulletin Board

Cut 1 bulletin board from 1/2" wood. Paint on design and coat with clear acrylic or polyurethane. Cut thin cork to fit the bottom of the board below the design.

1 square = 1"

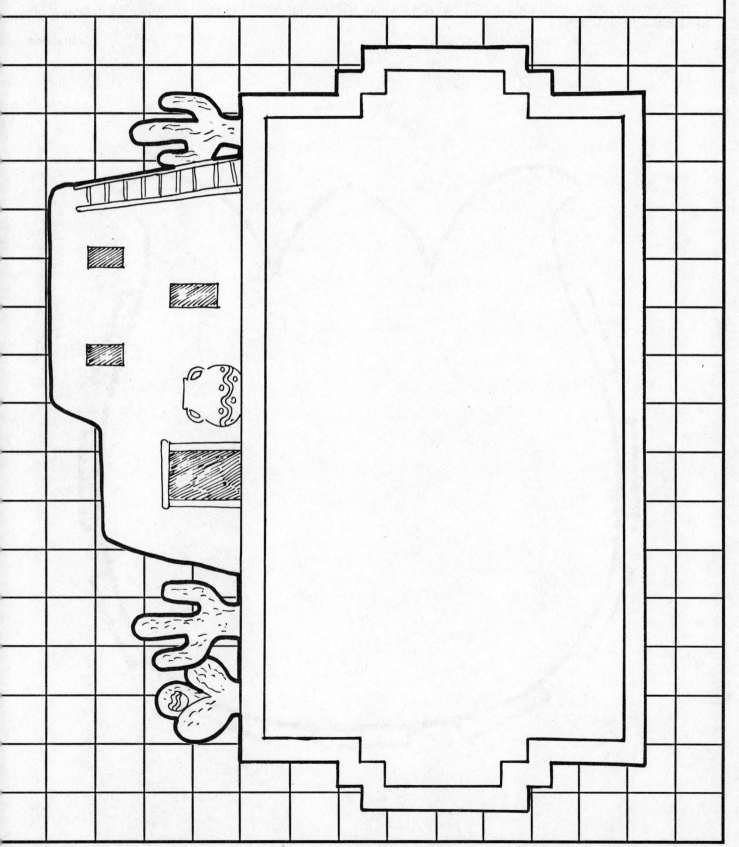

Tulip Slat Basket

Cut 2 tulip side pieces and 9 slats (slats should be cut from 1/2" lathing). Make the slats approximately 8" long. Paint and coat with clear acrylic.

Actual Size

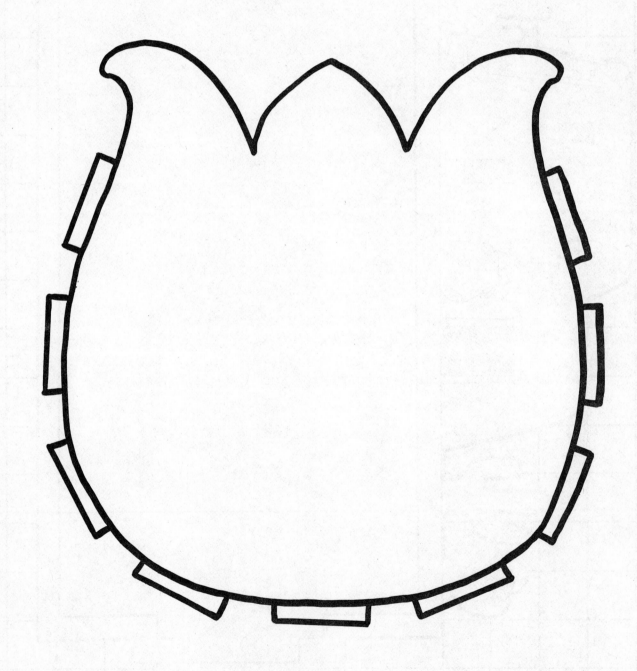

Victorian Figures

Cut figures from 3/4" wood. Figures may stand alone or a base may be added. (There is no standard pattern for bases.) Combinations of figures may be used to create a unique decoration. Use floral fabrics or wallpaper, real lace and dried flowers, if desired, to finish. Use muted colors. Coat with clear acrylic.

1 square = 1"

Victorian Figures
(Continued from previous page)
1 square = 1"

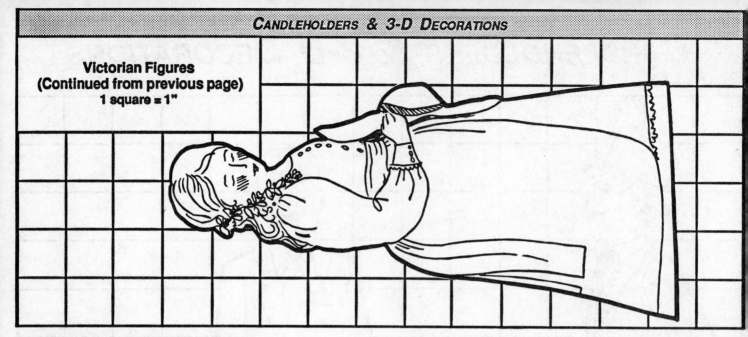

1920's Man and Woman Busts

Cut out bust and stand for each piece from 3/4" wood. Assemble with a wood screw from the bottom of the base. Paint as indicated.

Actual Size

Double Heart Candle Stand

Cut 1 each of the 2 hearts and 1 stand from 1/2" or 3/4" wood. Drill holes for candles in the hearts as indicated. Attach the hearts to the base as indicated by the arrow. Paint as indicated and coat with clear acrylic.   **1 square = 1"**

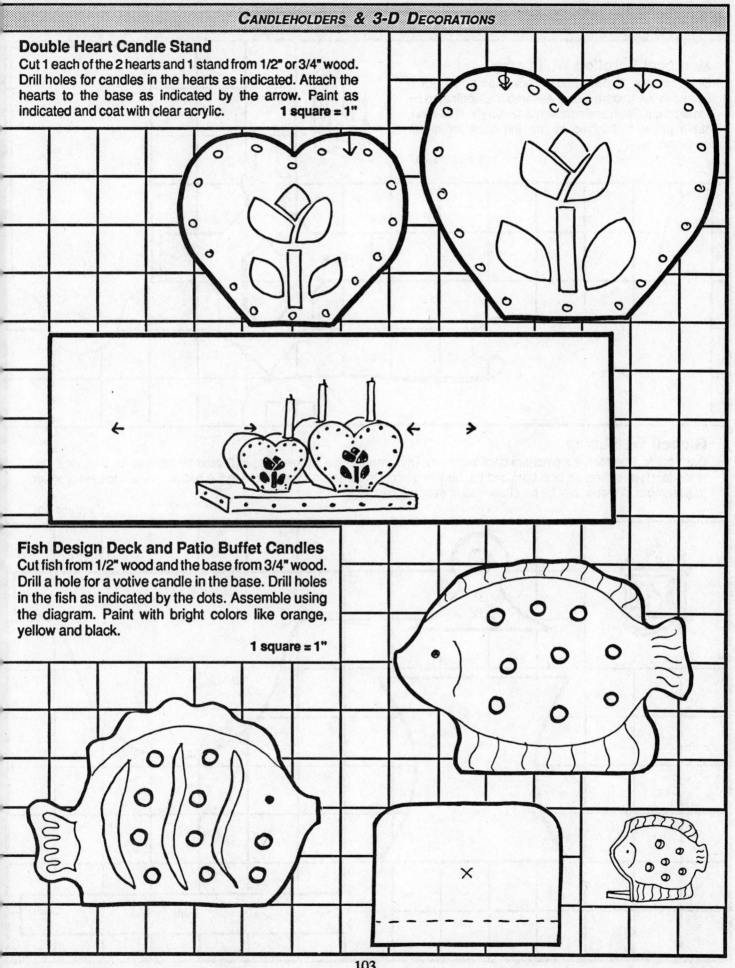

Fish Design Deck and Patio Buffet Candles

Cut fish from 1/2" wood and the base from 3/4" wood. Drill a hole for a votive candle in the base. Drill holes in the fish as indicated by the dots. Assemble using the diagram. Paint with bright colors like orange, yellow and black.

1 square = 1"

Medieval Scrolled Wall Lamp

Cut 1 bottom, 2 sides and 1 back. Drill a hole for a candle in the bottom piece. Assemble as indicated by the diagram. Stain and coat with clear acrylic. If desired, cut a piece of flashing to line the back for better illumination.

1 square = 1"

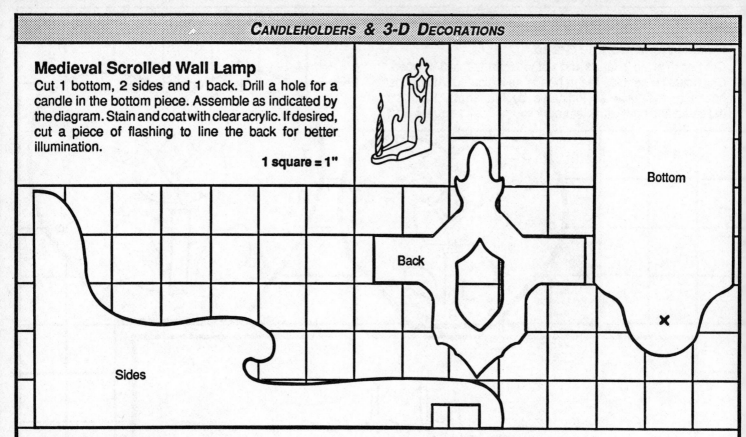

Globed Wall Lamp

Cut 1 back, 1 bottom, 2 top/bottom bars and 1 top. Drill a hole in the top piece as indicated by the hole for a hanger. Drill holes for dowels through both bars and the bottom piece. Drill a hole for the candle in the bottom piece. Use the diagram to assemble. A globe may be purchased to fit over the candle.

1 square = 1"

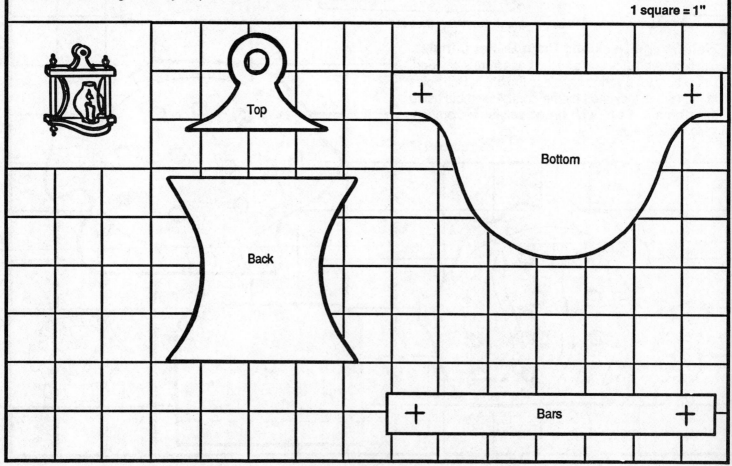

Rolling Primitive Spotted Bunny

Cut 1 bunny and 2 wheels. Wheels may be attached with screws, or they may be drilled to insert a small dowel. The spots are outlined and should be painted with your choice of colors.

Actual Size

3-D Cat

Cut 1 body, 1 tail, 1 heart and 1 brace. Dotted lines show cutting lines for heart and tail. Assemble as indicated. Attach the brace to the center back for a stand with wood glue.

Actual Size

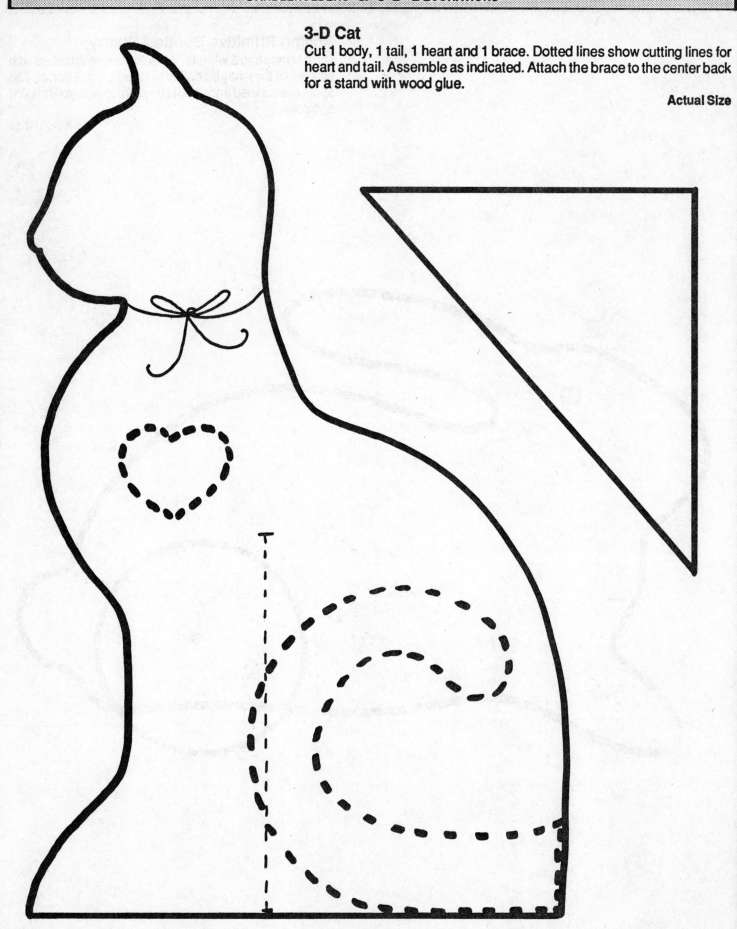

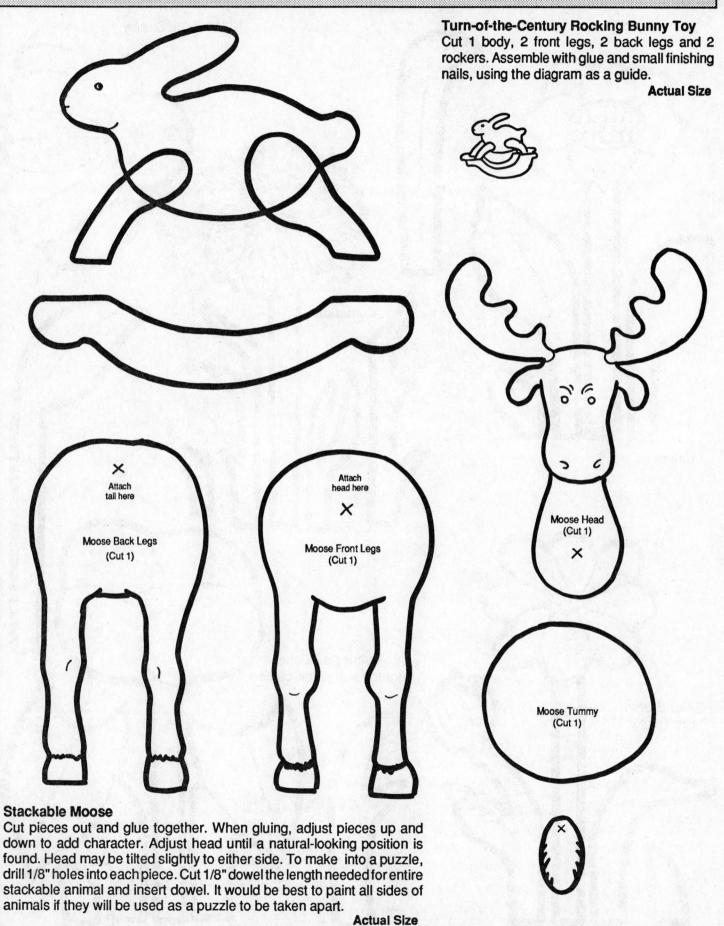

Turn-of-the-Century Rocking Bunny Toy
Cut 1 body, 2 front legs, 2 back legs and 2 rockers. Assemble with glue and small finishing nails, using the diagram as a guide.

Actual Size

Attach
tail here

Moose Back Legs
(Cut 1)

Attach
head here

Moose Front Legs
(Cut 1)

Moose Head
(Cut 1)

Moose Tummy
(Cut 1)

Stackable Moose
Cut pieces out and glue together. When gluing, adjust pieces up and down to add character. Adjust head until a natural-looking position is found. Head may be tilted slightly to either side. To make into a puzzle, drill 1/8" holes into each piece. Cut 1/8" dowel the length needed for entire stackable animal and insert dowel. It would be best to paint all sides of animals if they will be used as a puzzle to be taken apart.

Actual Size

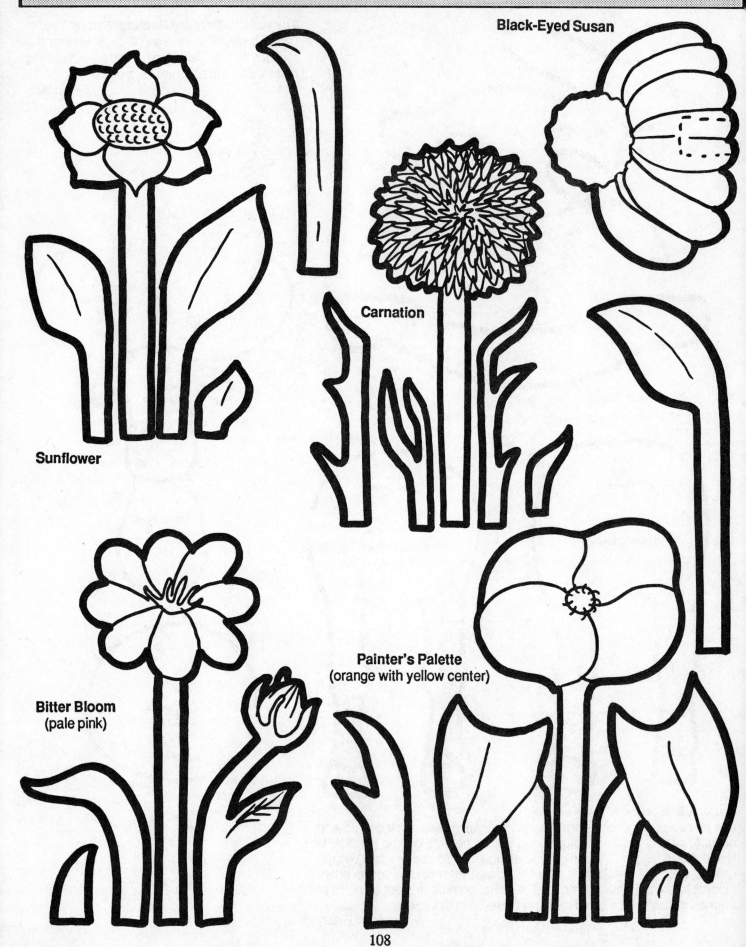

Black-Eyed Susan

Carnation

Sunflower

Bitter Bloom
(pale pink)

Painter's Palette
(orange with yellow center)

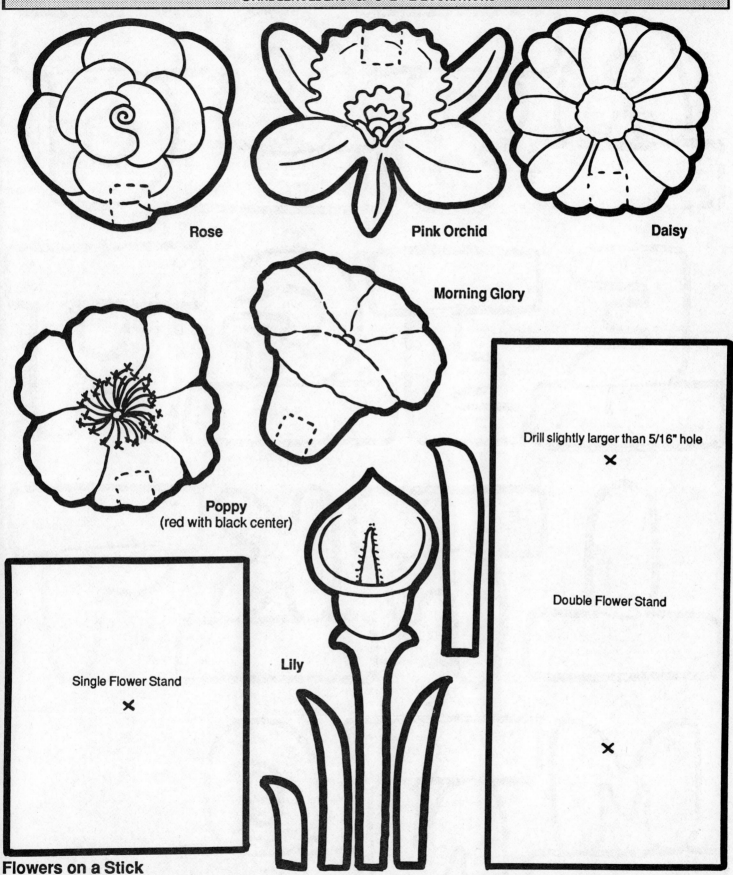

Rose

Pink Orchid

Daisy

Morning Glory

Drill slightly larger than 5/16" hole

✕

Double Flower Stand

✕

Poppy
(red with black center)

Single Flower Stand

✕

Lily

Flowers on a Stick

Directions: Cut out blooms, glue 5/16" dowel in holes for stems. Dowel may be spray painted green if desired. Flowers may be placed in a vase, on stands (patterns included), or tie a bow around the stem and give as gifts or party favors. If using stands, stems may vary to desired lengths.

Actual Size

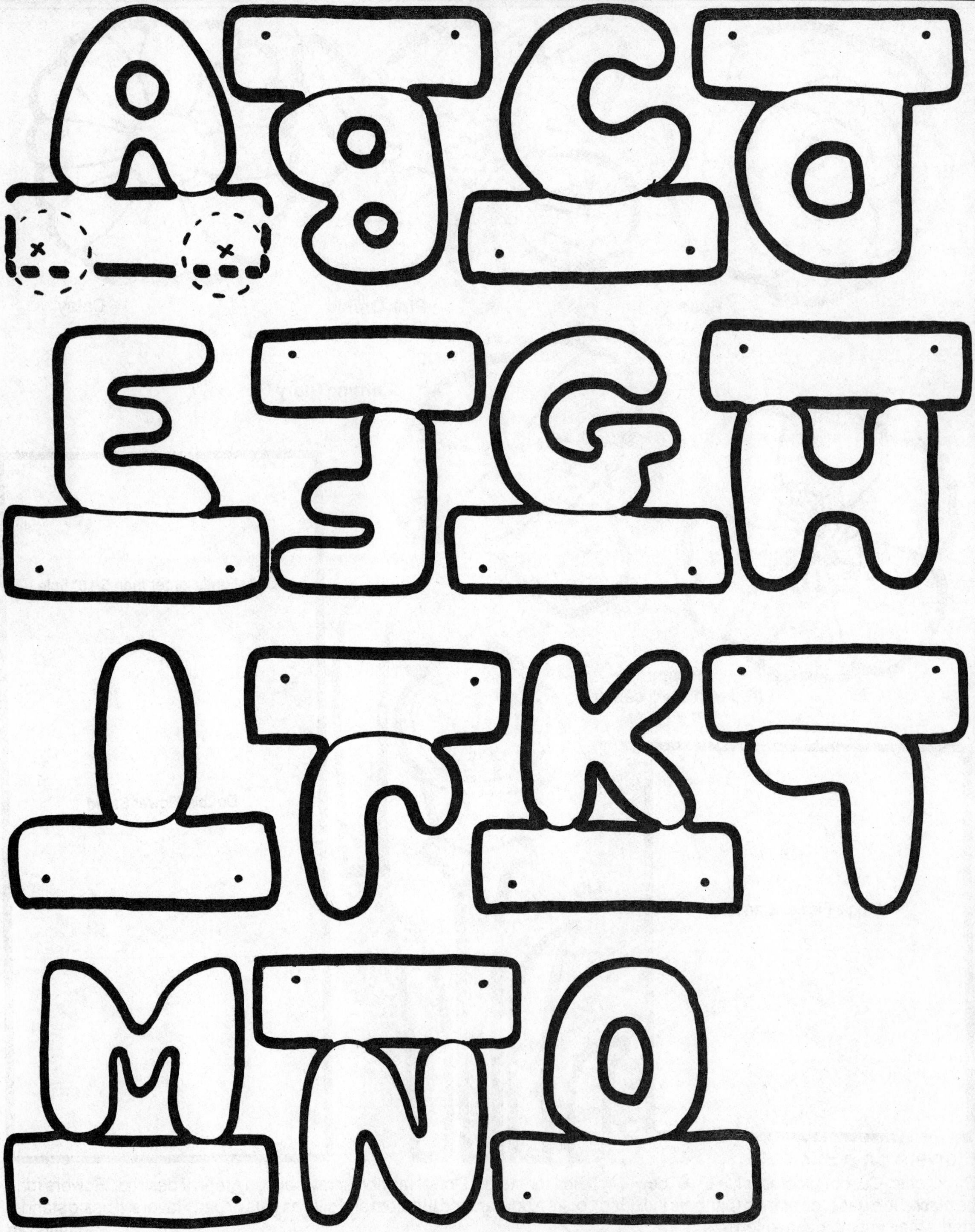

coal

P Q R S T U

Spell Your Name Train
Cut out 1 train engine, 1 coal car, 1 caboose and as many letters as you need. Cut 4 wheels for each piece, as indicated by the pattern. Attach eyes and hooks (or just eyes and tie yarn, leather or twine between each car or letter. Attach wheels with screws or drill for small dowels. Paint in bright colors. Use for names, messages (I love you, I miss you, etc.) or phrases (Mary + Paul).

Actual Size

Jointed Honey Bear

Cut 1 bear body, 2 arms, 2 legs and 1 honey pot. Drill holes in arms, legs and through the body to insert dowels so that the bear is movable. The honey pot is to set alongside the bear. Paint as indicated and coat with clear acrylic.

Actual Size

HONEY

Three Bear Chunkies
Cut each stand-along figure from 1-1/2" wood.
Paint as indicated. Coat with clear acrylic.

1 square = 3/4"

Swinging Leg Bunny

Cut 1 bunny and 2 legs from 3/4" wood. Drill hole completely through the side, as shown, to insert a small dowel or metal rod to attach legs. Finish as indicated or glue on or sew fabric clothes.

Actual Size

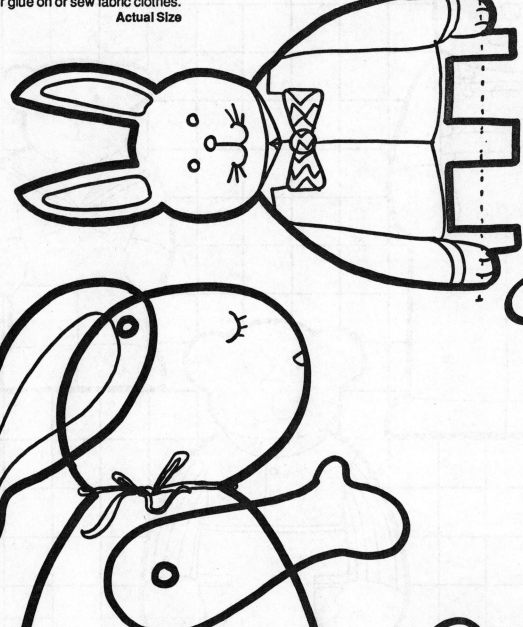

Floppy Eared Jointed Bunny

Cut 1 body, 2 arms, 2 legs and 2 ears. Drill as indicated to insert dowels to make pieces movable. Paint as indicated and tie twine around the bunny's neck.

Actual Size

3-D Mouse

Cut out 1 body and 2 back legs from 1/2" wood. Cut 2 front legs and 1 set of ears from 1/4" wood. Assemble and paint gray with black detailing.

Actual Size

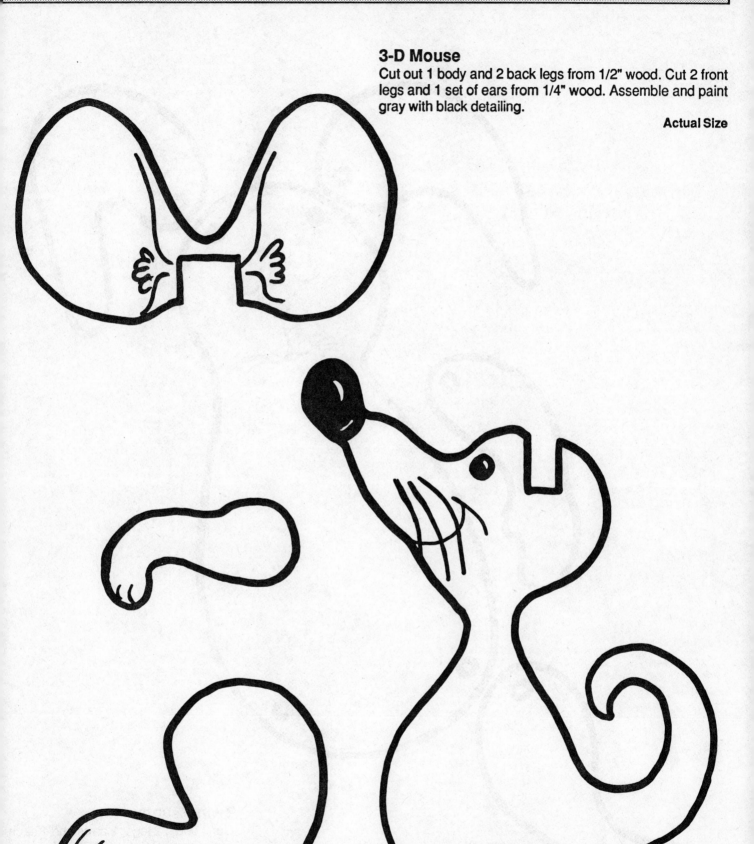

Twine Bunny
Cut 1 body, 2 legs, 2 arms and 1 each of the ears. Paint as indicated and tie limbs on with twine. (The twine should be tied into a bow at each joint.)
Actual Size

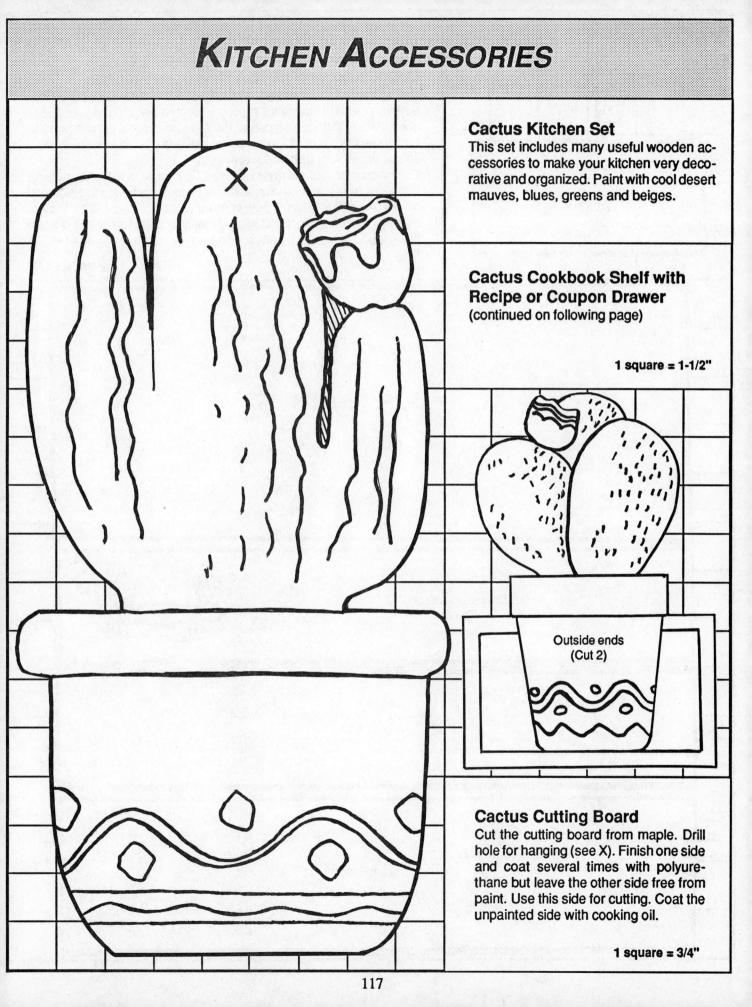

Cactus Kitchen Set

This set includes many useful wooden accessories to make your kitchen very decorative and organized. Paint with cool desert mauves, blues, greens and beiges.

Cactus Cookbook Shelf with Recipe or Coupon Drawer

(continued on following page)

1 square = 1-1/2"

Outside ends
(Cut 2)

Cactus Cutting Board

Cut the cutting board from maple. Drill hole for hanging (see X). Finish one side and coat several times with polyurethane but leave the other side free from paint. Use this side for cutting. Coat the unpainted side with cooking oil.

1 square = 3/4"

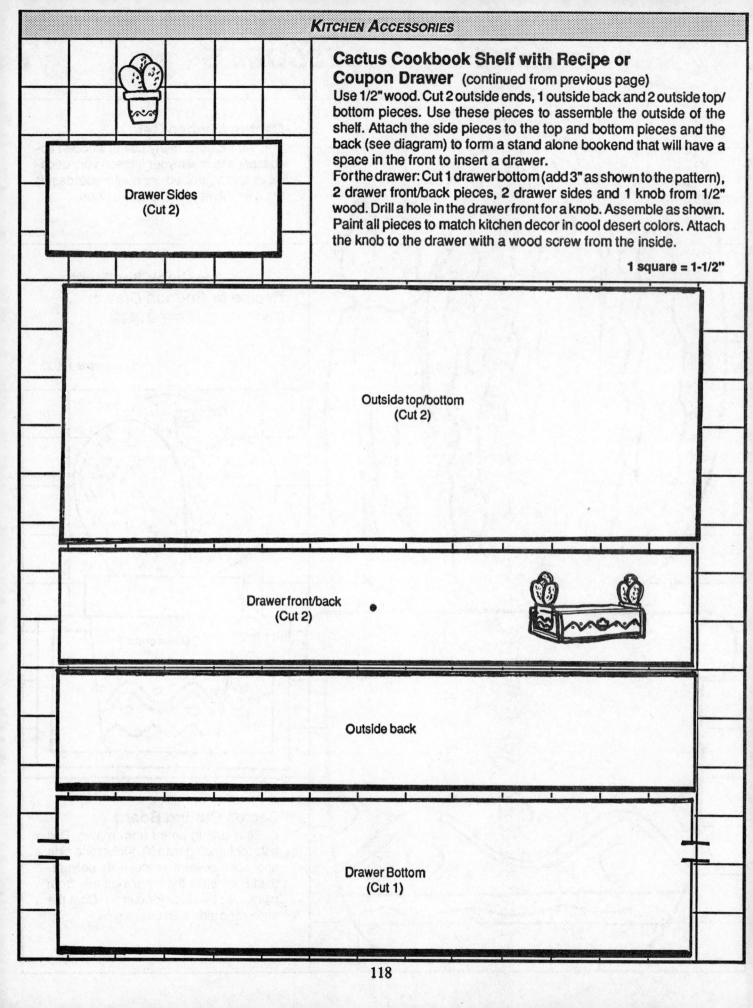

Drawer Sides
(Cut 2)

Cactus Cookbook Shelf with Recipe or Coupon Drawer (continued from previous page)

Use 1/2" wood. Cut 2 outside ends, 1 outside back and 2 outside top/bottom pieces. Use these pieces to assemble the outside of the shelf. Attach the side pieces to the top and bottom pieces and the back (see diagram) to form a stand alone bookend that will have a space in the front to insert a drawer.

For the drawer: Cut 1 drawer bottom (add 3" as shown to the pattern), 2 drawer front/back pieces, 2 drawer sides and 1 knob from 1/2" wood. Drill a hole in the drawer front for a knob. Assemble as shown. Paint all pieces to match kitchen decor in cool desert colors. Attach the knob to the drawer with a wood screw from the inside.

1 square = 1-1/2"

Outside top/bottom
(Cut 2)

Drawer front/back
(Cut 2)

Outside back

Drawer Bottom
(Cut 1)

118

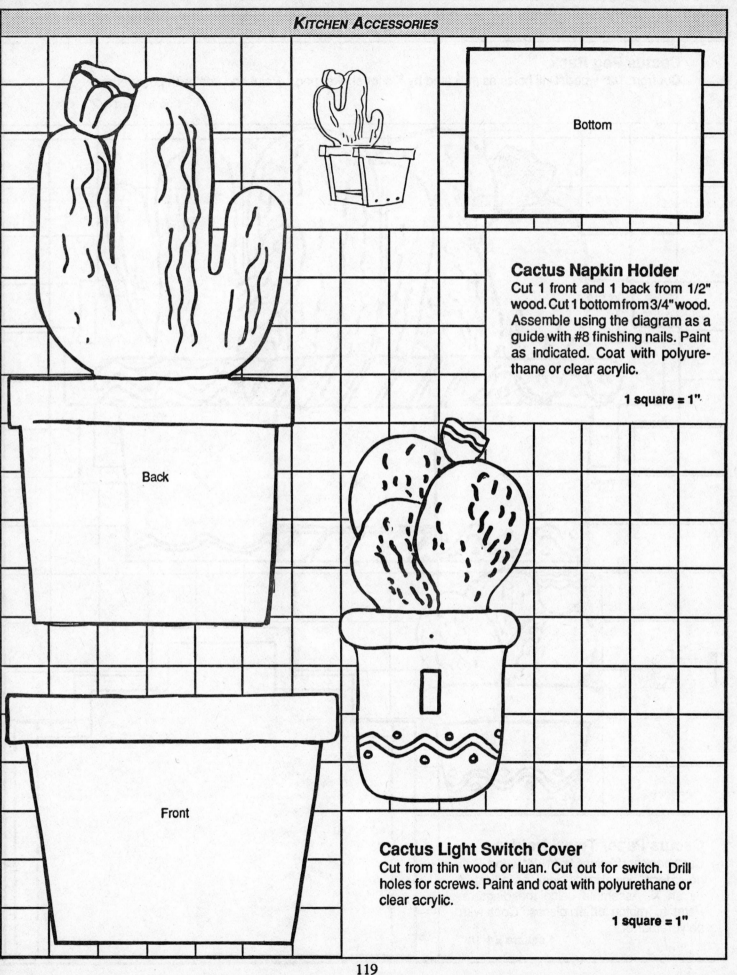

Bottom

Cactus Napkin Holder

Cut 1 front and 1 back from 1/2"
wood. Cut 1 bottom from 3/4" wood.
Assemble using the diagram as a
guide with #8 finishing nails. Paint
as indicated. Coat with polyurethane or clear acrylic.

1 square = 1"

Back

Front

Cactus Light Switch Cover

Cut from thin wood or luan. Cut out for switch. Drill
holes for screws. Paint and coat with polyurethane or
clear acrylic.

1 square = 1"

Cactus Peg Rack

Cut from 1/2" wood. Drill holes as indicated by X's for shaker pegs. Paint and coat with polyurethane.

1 square = 1-1/2"

Cactus Paper Towel Holder

Cut 1 back and 2 sides from 3/4" wood. Drill holes for 1" dowel in the sides, as indicated by an X. Assemble using the diagram. Paint to match other pieces. Coat with polyurethane.

1 square = 1-1/2"

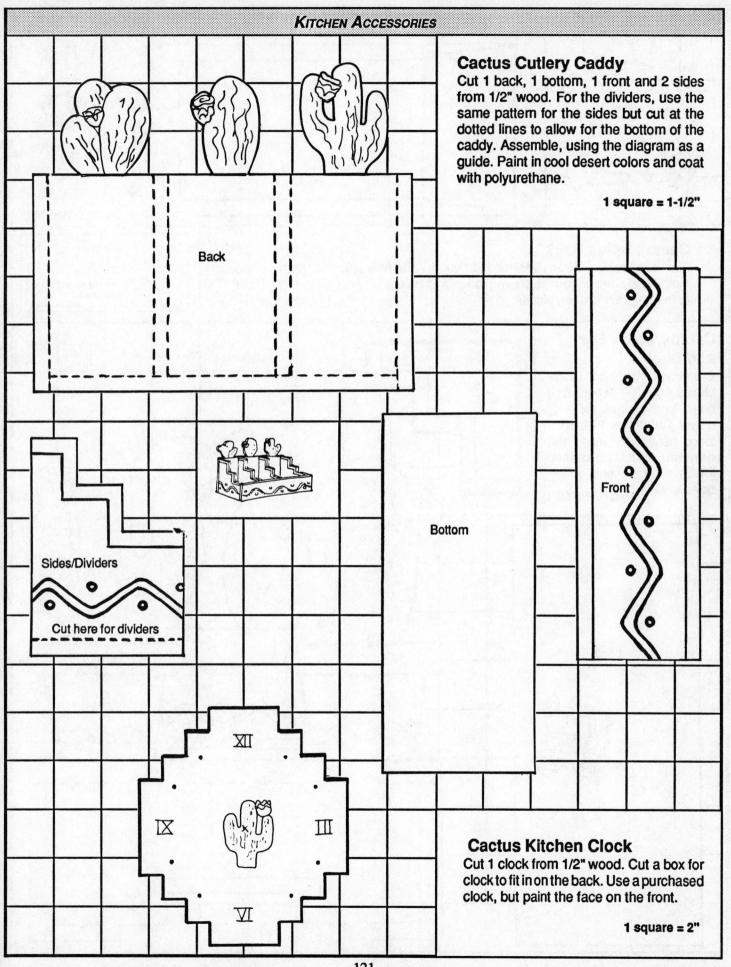

Cactus Cutlery Caddy

Cut 1 back, 1 bottom, 1 front and 2 sides from 1/2" wood. For the dividers, use the same pattern for the sides but cut at the dotted lines to allow for the bottom of the caddy. Assemble, using the diagram as a guide. Paint in cool desert colors and coat with polyurethane.

1 square = 1-1/2"

Back

Sides/Dividers

Cut here for dividers

Bottom

Front

XII

IX   III

VI

Cactus Kitchen Clock

Cut 1 clock from 1/2" wood. Cut a box for clock to fit in on the back. Use a purchased clock, but paint the face on the front.

1 square = 2"

121

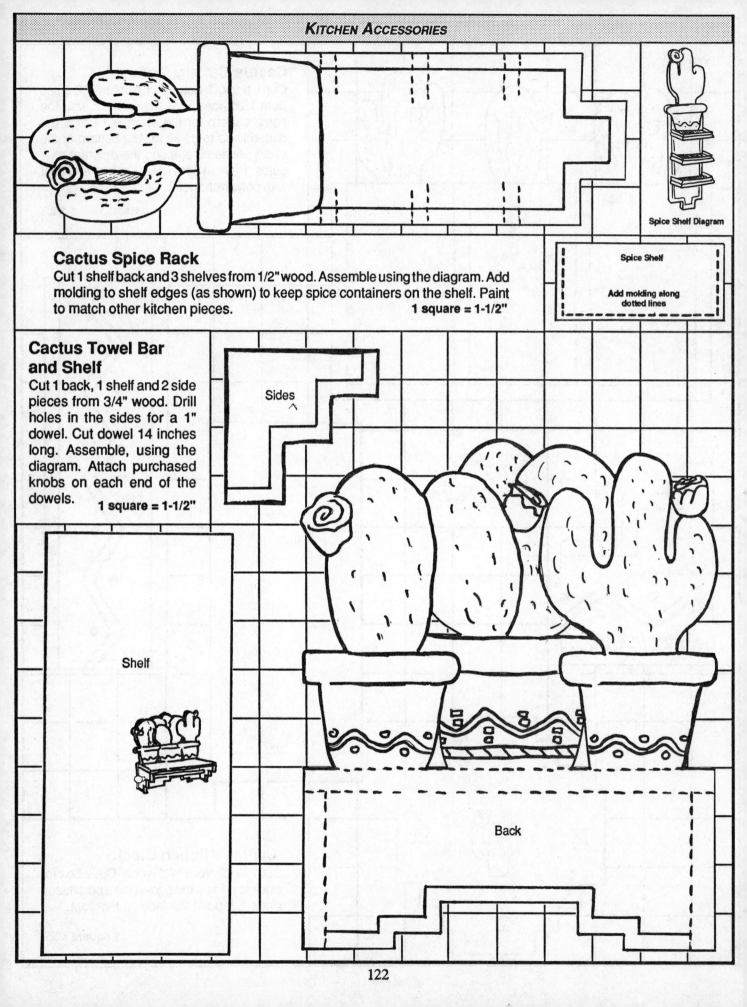

Spice Shelf Diagram

Spice Shelf

Add molding along
dotted lines

Cactus Spice Rack

Cut 1 shelf back and 3 shelves from 1/2" wood. Assemble using the diagram. Add molding to shelf edges (as shown) to keep spice containers on the shelf. Paint to match other kitchen pieces.

1 square = 1-1/2"

Cactus Towel Bar and Shelf

Cut 1 back, 1 shelf and 2 side pieces from 3/4" wood. Drill holes in the sides for a 1" dowel. Cut dowel 14 inches long. Assemble, using the diagram. Attach purchased knobs on each end of the dowels.

1 square = 1-1/2"

Sides

Shelf

Back

Napkin Rings

Cut as many napkin ring squares as desired from 3/4" wood. Cut center circle from these squares. Choose a napkin ring motif and cut out as many as needed from thin wood. Paint as indicated by pattern to match kitchen decor. Glue the motifs to the top of the napkin rings. Paint with polyurethane or clear acrylic.

Actual Size

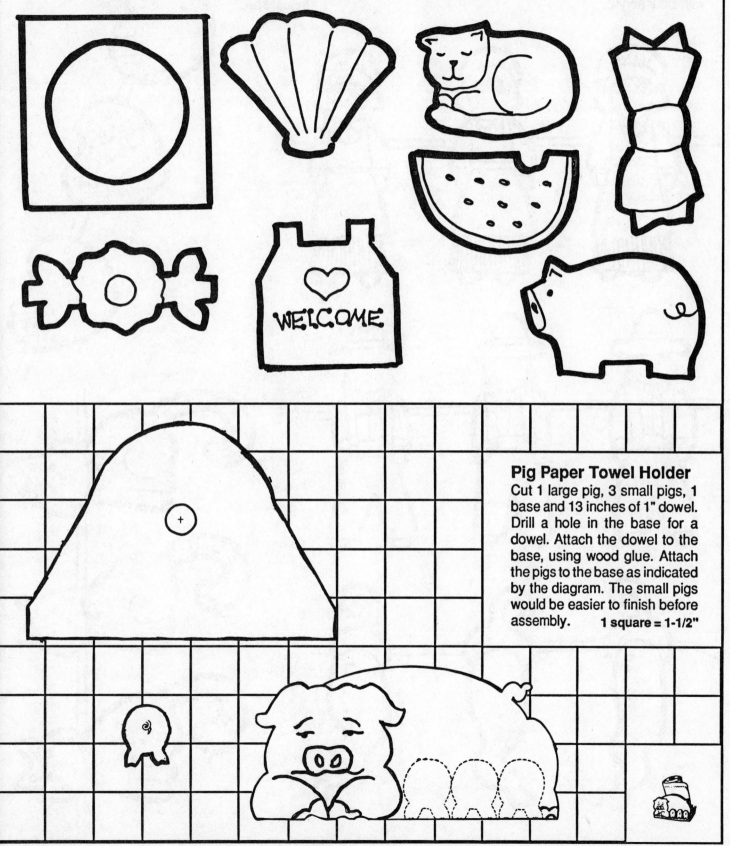

Pig Paper Towel Holder

Cut 1 large pig, 3 small pigs, 1 base and 13 inches of 1" dowel. Drill a hole in the base for a dowel. Attach the dowel to the base, using wood glue. Attach the pigs to the base as indicated by the diagram. The small pigs would be easier to finish before assembly.   **1 square = 1-1/2"**

Kitchen Chair-Back Garlands

Cut enough of each garland motif to drape between the posts of ladderback chairs. Leave enough jute or ribbon at the ends to tie in a bow on chair posts. Motifs may be mixed (i.e. bear, heart, bear, etc.). Paint before stringing and coat with clear acrylic.

Actual Size

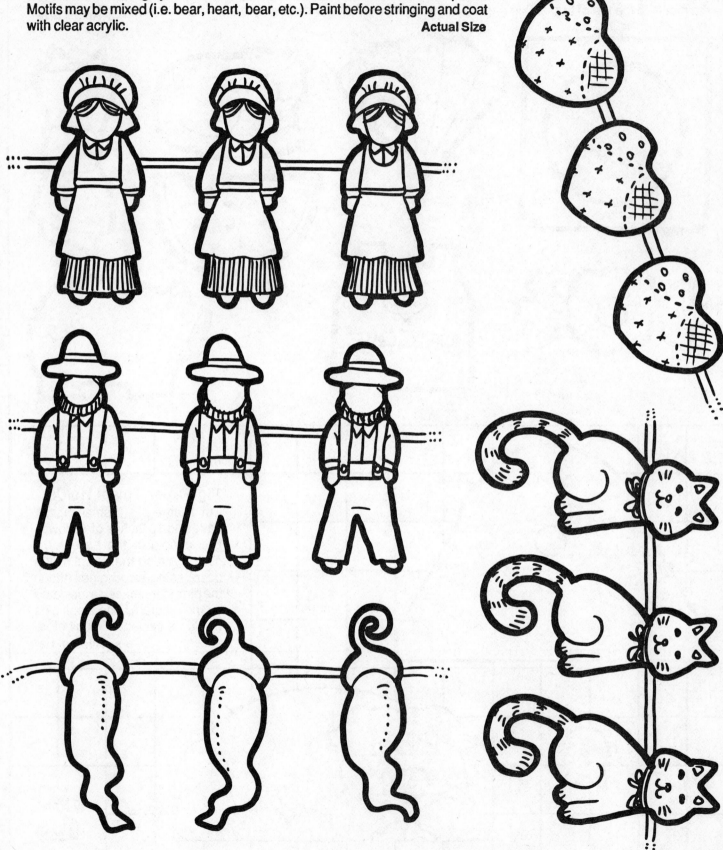

Tulip Design Bathroom Set

Tulip Double Peg Rack

Cut from 3/4" wood. Drill holes where indicated by an X for shaker pegs. Paint to match bathroom decor. Attach a hanger to the back. Coat with polyurethane.

Actual Size

Tulip Bathroom
Tissue Paper Holder

Cut 1 brace from 1/2" wood and 2 side pieces from 3/4" wood. Cut a 1" dowel, 7" long. The dotted lines on the side piece indicate the placement of the brace, and the X indicates where to drill for the dowel. Drill holes in the side pieces for the dowel. (The holes for the dowel must be drilled all the way through the side pieces.) Assemble using diagram as a guide. Paint to match bathroom decor and coat with polyurethane. Attach to the bathroom wall to studs with wood screws.

Actual Size

Bathroom Tissue Paper Brace

WELCOME

Tulip Bathroom Clock
Follow directions given in the clock section. Paint to match bathroom decor. This clock was designed for a 4-1/2"
clock face.   **1 square = 3/4"**

Tulip Bathroom Shelves

Cut 2 side pieces from 3/4" wood and the 2 shelves from 1/2" wood. The dotted lines on the side pieces indicate the placement of shelves. Assemble using the diagram. Paint with acrylics to match your bathroom decor and coat with polyurethane. The shelves are on this page, the side pattern is on page 129.

1 square = 1"

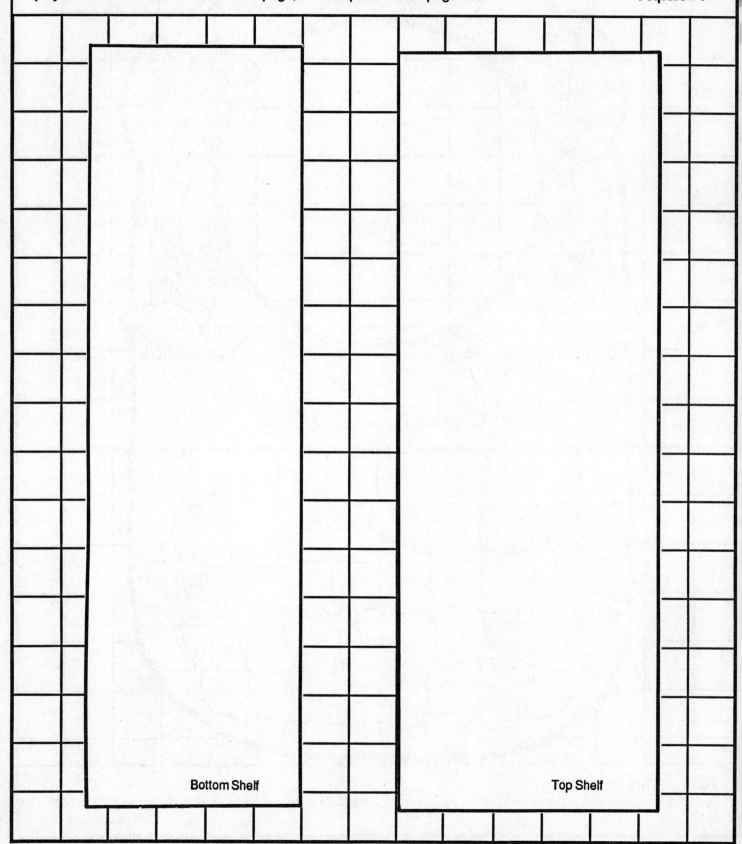

Bottom Shelf

Top Shelf

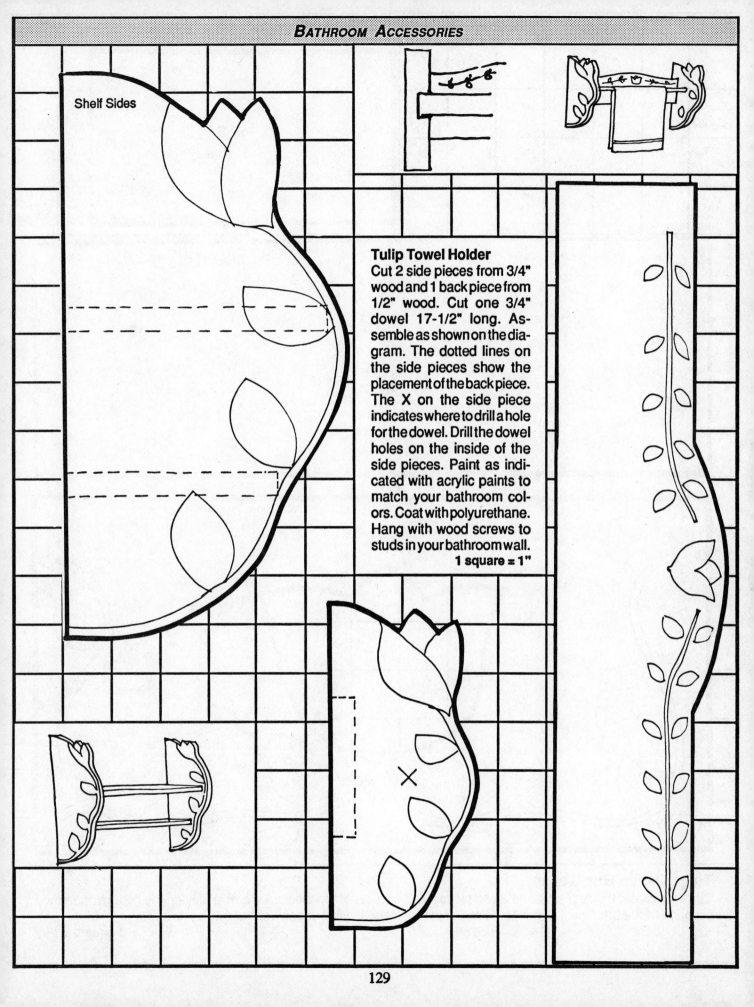

Shelf Sides

Tulip Towel Holder

Cut 2 side pieces from 3/4" wood and 1 back piece from 1/2" wood. Cut one 3/4" dowel 17-1/2" long. Assemble as shown on the diagram. The dotted lines on the side pieces show the placement of the back piece. The X on the side piece indicates where to drill a hole for the dowel. Drill the dowel holes on the inside of the side pieces. Paint as indicated with acrylic paints to match your bathroom colors. Coat with polyurethane. Hang with wood screws to studs in your bathroom wall.

1 square = 1"

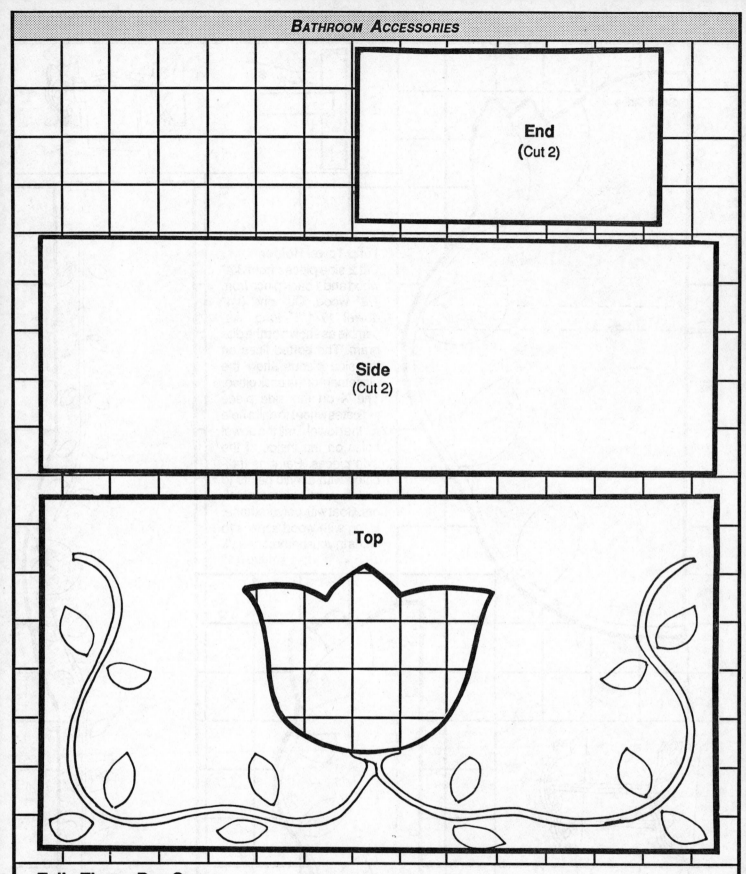

End
(Cut 2)

Side
(Cut 2)

Top

Tulip Tissue Box Cover
Cut 1 top piece, 2 side pieces and 2 end pieces. Cut tulip out of top piece. Assemble leaving the bottom open for covering tissue box. Paint as indicated and coat with clear acrylics or polyurethane.

1 square = 3/4"

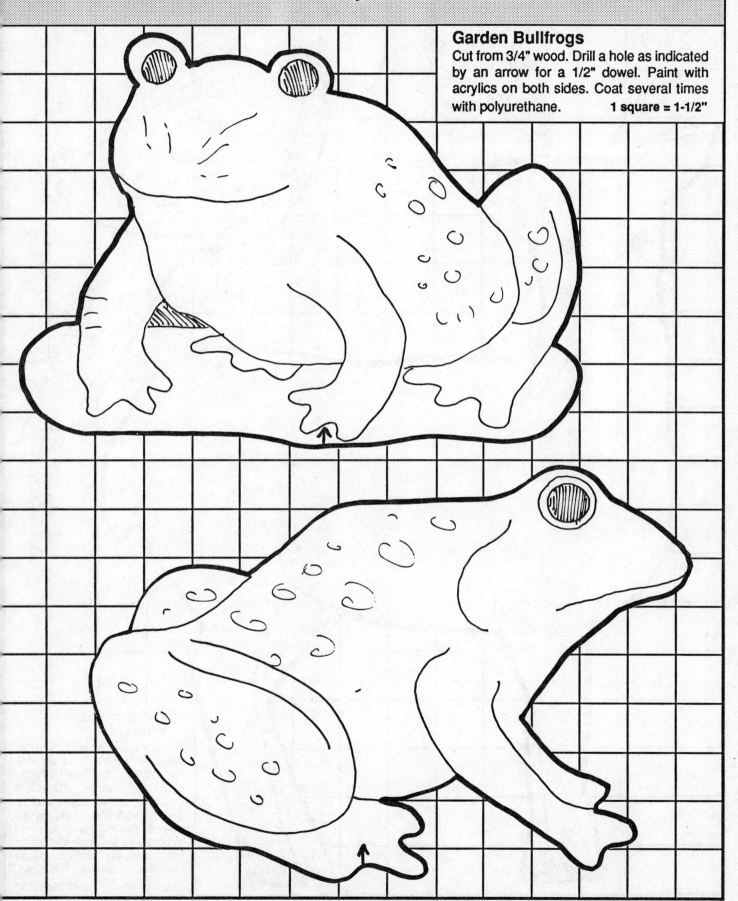

Garden Bullfrogs
Cut from 3/4" wood. Drill a hole as indicated by an arrow for a 1/2" dowel. Paint with acrylics on both sides. Coat several times with polyurethane.   **1 square = 1-1/2"**

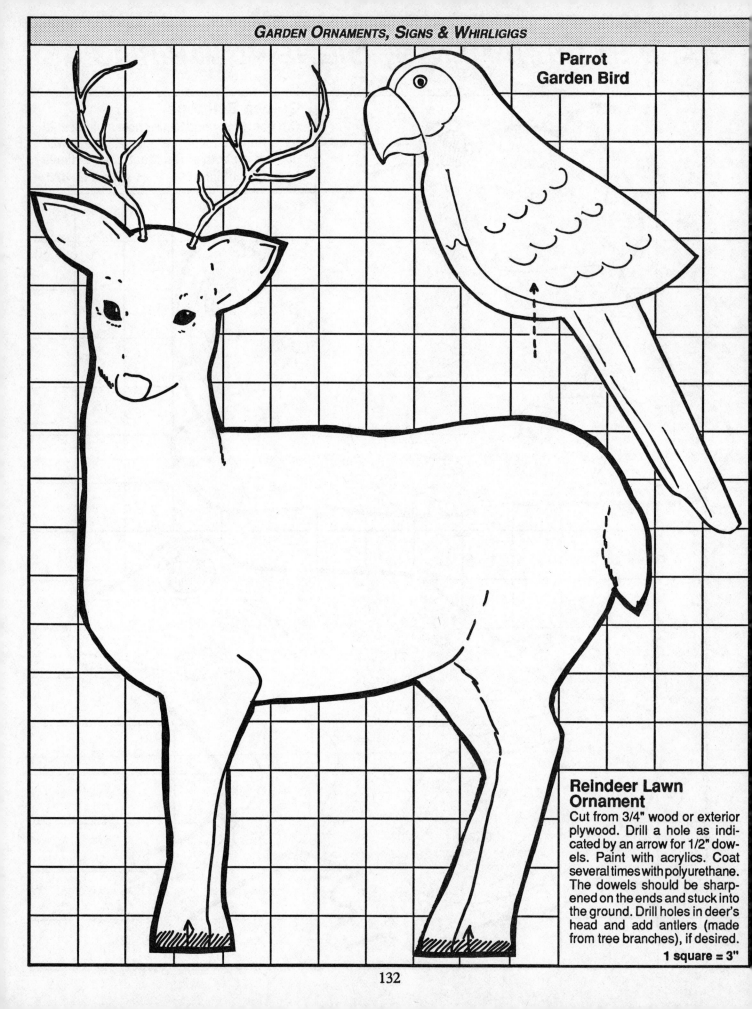

Parrot Garden Bird

Reindeer Lawn Ornament

Cut from 3/4" wood or exterior plywood. Drill a hole as indicated by an arrow for 1/2" dowels. Paint with acrylics. Coat several times with polyurethane. The dowels should be sharpened on the ends and stuck into the ground. Drill holes in deer's head and add antlers (made from tree branches), if desired.

1 square = 3"

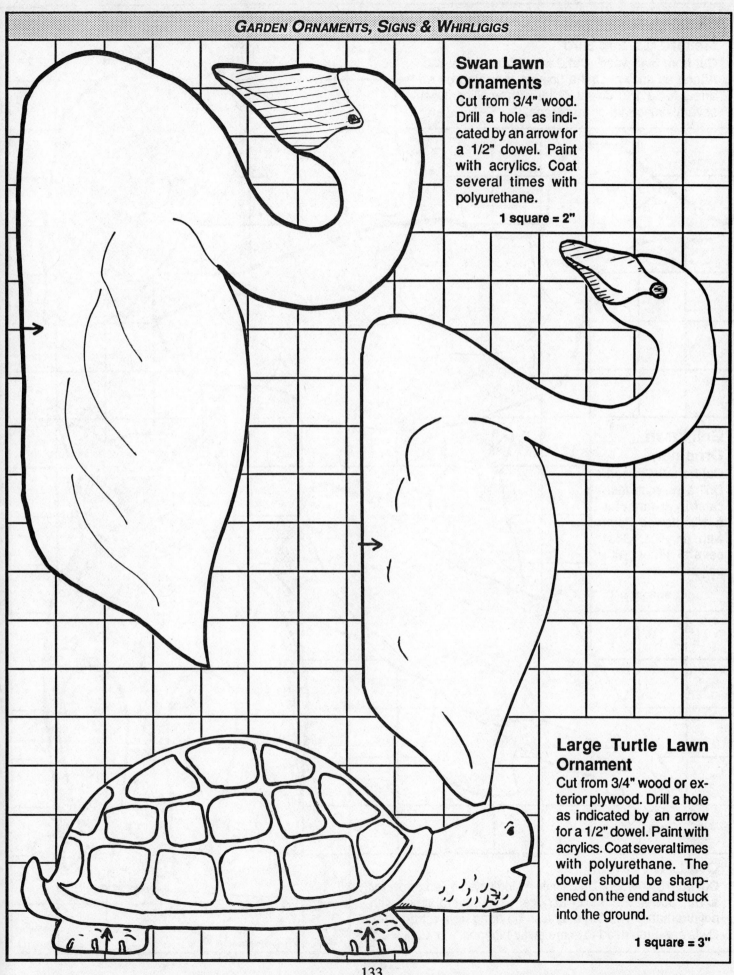

Swan Lawn Ornaments

Cut from 3/4" wood. Drill a hole as indicated by an arrow for a 1/2" dowel. Paint with acrylics. Coat several times with polyurethane.

1 square = 2"

Large Turtle Lawn Ornament

Cut from 3/4" wood or exterior plywood. Drill a hole as indicated by an arrow for a 1/2" dowel. Paint with acrylics. Coat several times with polyurethane. The dowel should be sharpened on the end and stuck into the ground.

1 square = 3"

Mallard Garden Bird

Cut from 3/4" wood. Cut 2 wings from thin wood. Attach as shown. Drill a hole as indicated by an arrow for a 1/2" dowel. Paint with acrylics. Coat several times with polyurethane.   **1 square = 1"**

Gull Lawn Ornament

Cut from 3/4" wood. Drill a hole as indicated by an arrow for a 1/2" dowel. Paint with acrylics. Coat several times with polyurethane.

1 square = 3"

Owl Lawn Ornament

Cut from 3/4" wood. Drill a hole as indicated by an arrow for a 1/2" dowel. Paint with acrylics. Coat several times with polyurethane. The owl may also be hung from a tree limb. Owls are often used to scare away pigeons.   **1 square = 3"**

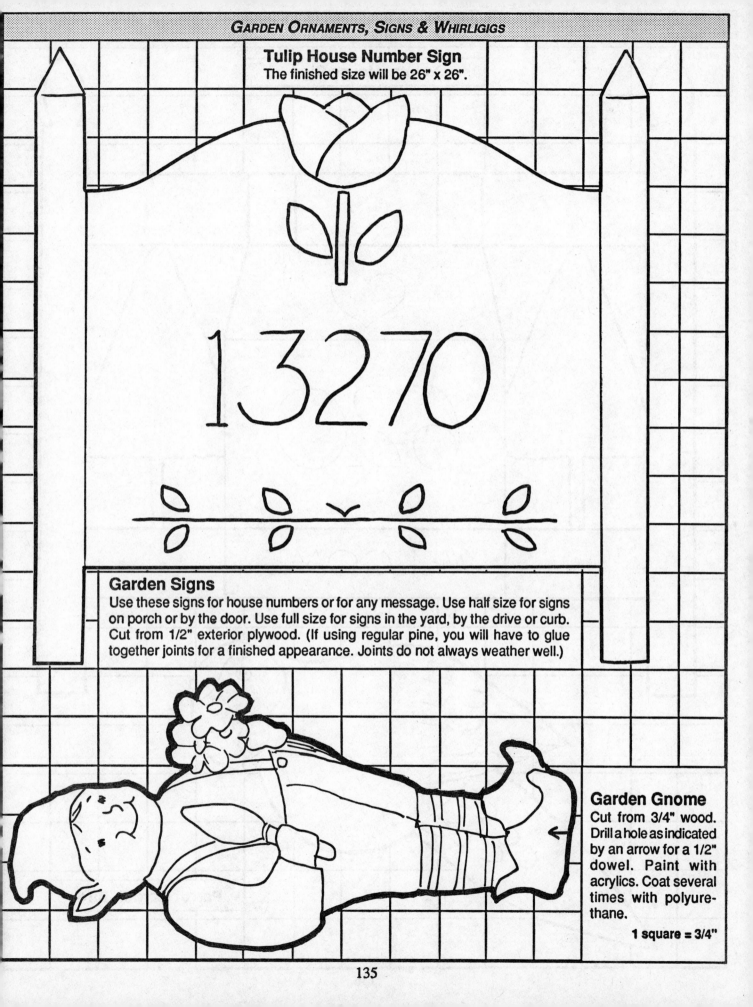

Tulip House Number Sign
The finished size will be 26" x 26".

13270

Garden Signs
Use these signs for house numbers or for any message. Use half size for signs on porch or by the door. Use full size for signs in the yard, by the drive or curb. Cut from 1/2" exterior plywood. (If using regular pine, you will have to glue together joints for a finished appearance. Joints do not always weather well.)

Garden Gnome
Cut from 3/4" wood. Drill a hole as indicated by an arrow for a 1/2" dowel. Paint with acrylics. Coat several times with polyurethane.

1 square = 3/4"

Country House Sign

620

WELCOME

Parrot Garden Bird

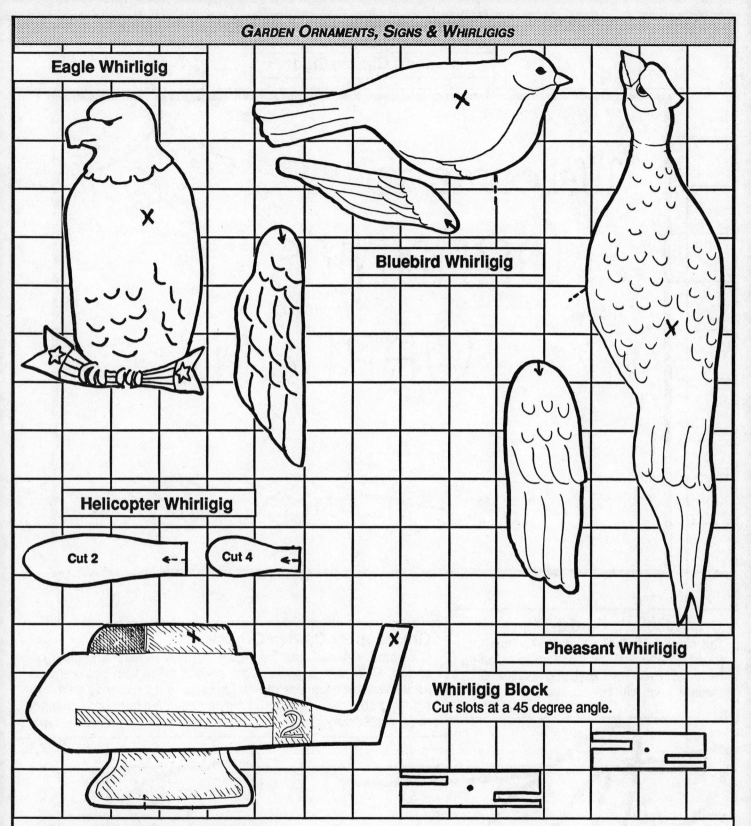

Eagle Whirligig

Bluebird Whirligig

Pheasant Whirligig

Helicopter Whirligig

Cut 2

Cut 4

Whirligig Block
Cut slots at a 45 degree angle.

Whirligig Assembly Instructions

Cut 1 whirligig body and 2 blocks from 3/4" wood. Cut blades from 1/8" wood. Cut slots at a 45 degree angle on each block end, perpendicular to the whirligig. Drill a hole for a 1/2" dowel through body of whirligig where indicated by an x. Insert a 1/2" dowel through the hole. Dowel should be cut long enough to extend blades away from the body so that they will twirl freely. Glue blades into wooden blocks with exterior glue and secure with a small finishing nail. Attach to dowel ends with metal washers and screw. Drill hole underneath whirligig and insert a 1/4" wooden (or metal) dowel. Drill hole for dowel into outside post and attach the whirligig to the post. This assembly will cause the whirligig to have some wind movement.

For all pattern pieces 1 square = 1"

Granny's Garden Sign

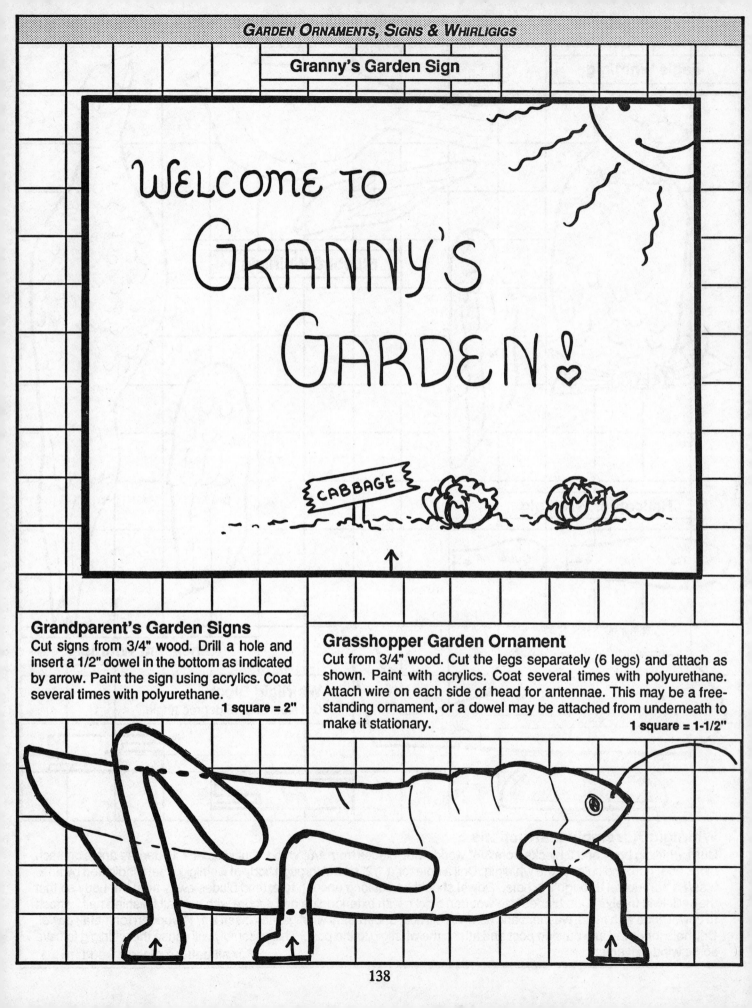

WELCOME TO GRANNY'S GARDEN! ♥

CABBAGE

Grandparent's Garden Signs

Cut signs from 3/4" wood. Drill a hole and insert a 1/2" dowel in the bottom as indicated by arrow. Paint the sign using acrylics. Coat several times with polyurethane.

1 square = 2"

Grasshopper Garden Ornament

Cut from 3/4" wood. Cut the legs separately (6 legs) and attach as shown. Paint with acrylics. Coat several times with polyurethane. Attach wire on each side of head for antennae. This may be a free-standing ornament, or a dowel may be attached from underneath to make it stationary.

1 square = 1-1/2"

Grandpa's Garden Sign

ENTERING

GRANDPA'S

GARDEN

(NO RABBITS ALLOWED!)

×

Base for Coyote Weather Vane

(on following page)

Farmer Goose
Garden Ornament

Cut out 1 goose, 2 wings, 1 set of feet. The pitchfork may be cut separately and attached between the wings or use a 1/2" dowel or broomstick for the pitchfork handle (a child's toy pitchfork may be used, if desired). Paint the goose on both sides. If this is to be used in the yard or garden, attach dowels or metal stakes to the feet to insert into the ground. If using on a porch, you may want to cut the feet from 1" wood so that the wind will not blow it over. Coat several times with polyurethane to prevent weathering.

1 square = 3"

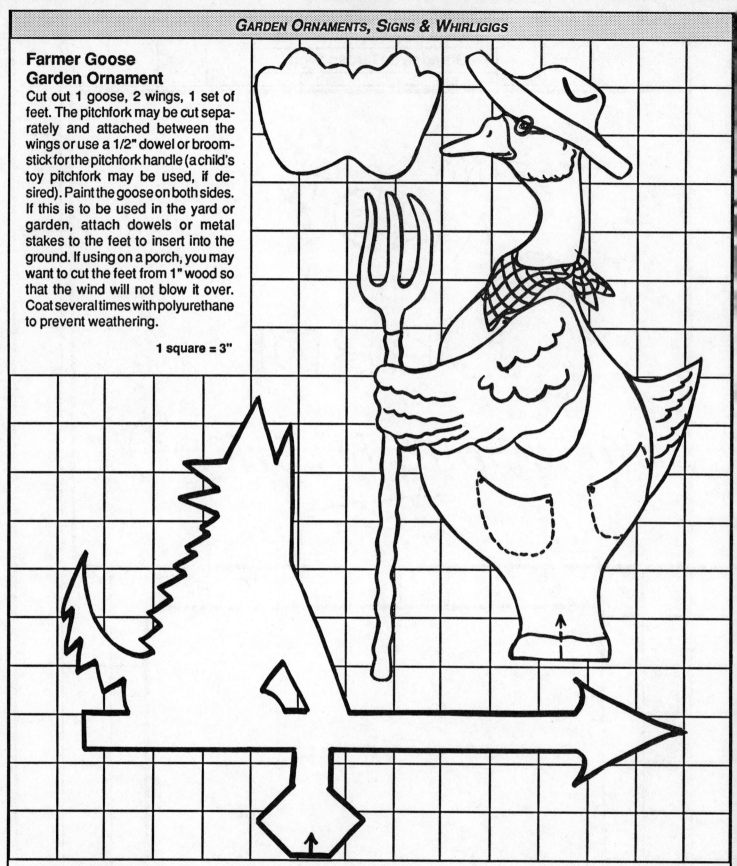

Coyote Weather Vane

Use as a weather vane or attach to the base and use for a decoration. Cut from 3/4" wood (hardwood would be more durable). Drill a hole as indicated for a 1/2" dowel. If using with the base, cut the dowel 7" long. Paint the coyote and arrow black for a silhouette. Coat several times with polyurethane. (Base on previous page.)

1 square = 3/4"

Country Welcome Garden Bunny
Cut from 3/4" wood. Drill a hole as indicated by
an arrow for a 1/2" dowel. Paint with acrylics.
Coat several times with polyurethane.

1 square = 3/4"

WELCOME FRIENDS

Pixie Garden Ornaments

Cut from 3/4" wood. Drill a hole as indicated by an arrow for a 1/2" dowel. Paint with acrylics. Coat several times with polyurethane.

1 square = 1"

Brownie Bird Feeder

Cut from 3/4" wood. Drill a hole as indicated by an arrow for a 1/2" dowel. Paint with acrylics. Coat several times with polyurethane. Using Plexiglas, cut a feeder bottom and 4 sides. Attach to the hand with a wood screw. A wooden bowl may be used instead but must be coated with polyurethane.   **1 square = 1"**

Watchful Cat Double Birdhouse

Cut 1 front piece, 2 side pieces 1 back piece and 2 middle/bottom pieces. Cut two 1-1/2" holes for bird to enter. Drill holes as indicated for two 3/8" x 3" dowels for a perch. Assemble, using the diagram as a guide.

1 square = 1-1/2"

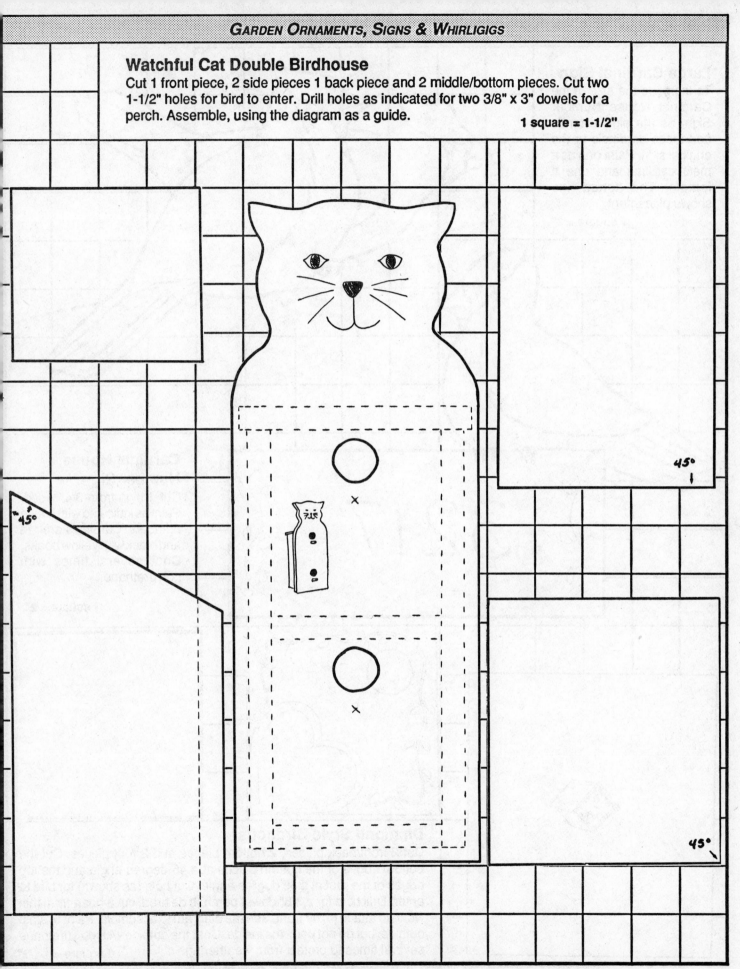

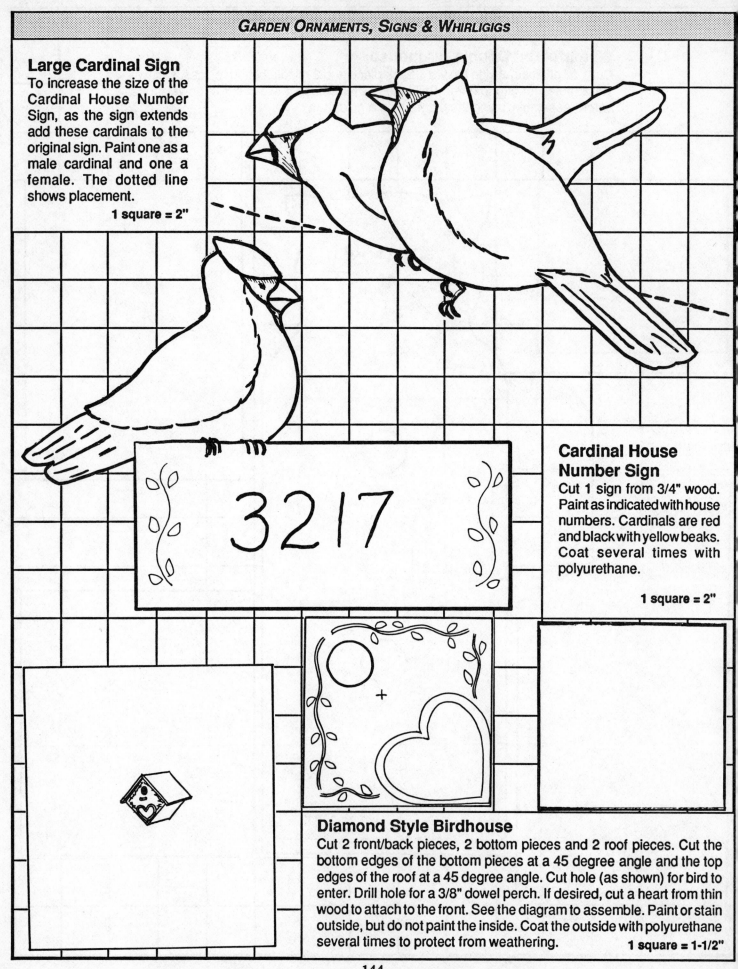

Large Cardinal Sign

To increase the size of the Cardinal House Number Sign, as the sign extends add these cardinals to the original sign. Paint one as a male cardinal and one a female. The dotted line shows placement.

1 square = 2"

Cardinal House Number Sign

Cut 1 sign from 3/4" wood. Paint as indicated with house numbers. Cardinals are red and black with yellow beaks. Coat several times with polyurethane.

1 square = 2"

3217

Diamond Style Birdhouse

Cut 2 front/back pieces, 2 bottom pieces and 2 roof pieces. Cut the bottom edges of the bottom pieces at a 45 degree angle and the top edges of the roof at a 45 degree angle. Cut hole (as shown) for bird to enter. Drill hole for a 3/8" dowel perch. If desired, cut a heart from thin wood to attach to the front. See the diagram to assemble. Paint or stain outside, but do not paint the inside. Coat the outside with polyurethane several times to protect from weathering.

1 square = 1-1/2"

Bunny & Tulip Fireplace Screen
Cut 1 screen and 2 screen bases. Assemble by attaching 1 base piece to each side of the screen (see diagram). Paint as indicated and coat with polyurethane.

1 square = 2"

Fancy Cutwork Screen

Cut 1 middle panel and 2 side panels. Cut out between tulips and heart in the center screen. Join together with three hinges equally spaced on each side. Approximate overall finished size of the middle screen is 55" x 18". Overall finished size of the sides is 48" x 14". Paint or stain. The designs may be routed, if desired. Coat with polyurethane. Use for a room divider or screen.   **1 square = 3"**

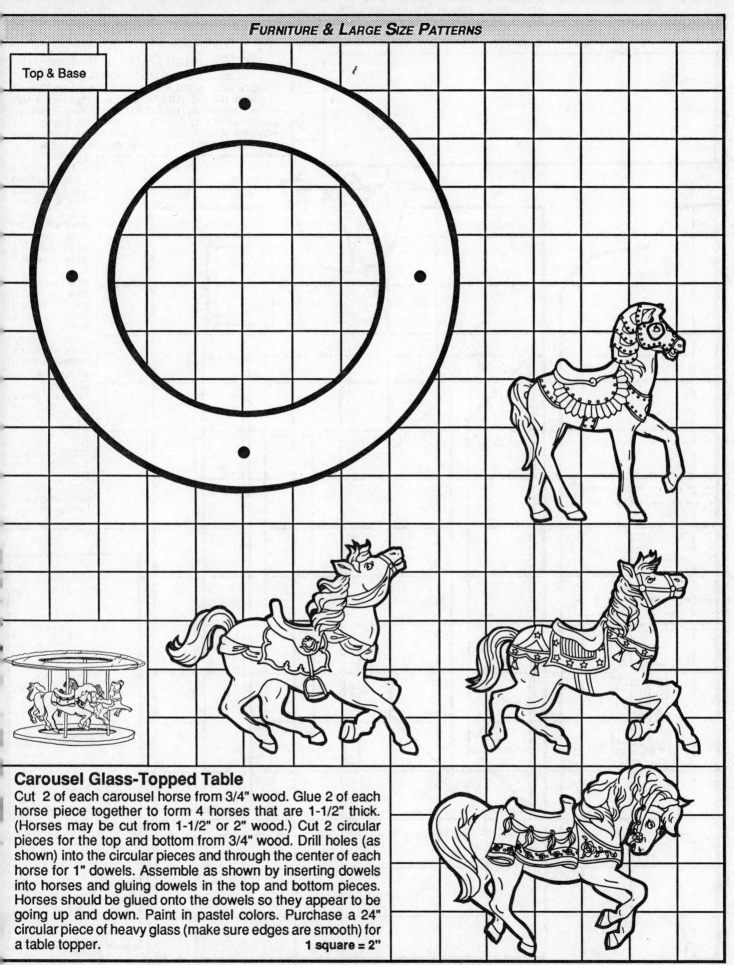

Top & Base

Carousel Glass-Topped Table

Cut 2 of each carousel horse from 3/4" wood. Glue 2 of each horse piece together to form 4 horses that are 1-1/2" thick. (Horses may be cut from 1-1/2" or 2" wood.) Cut 2 circular pieces for the top and bottom from 3/4" wood. Drill holes (as shown) into the circular pieces and through the center of each horse for 1" dowels. Assemble as shown by inserting dowels into horses and gluing dowels in the top and bottom pieces. Horses should be glued onto the dowels so they appear to be going up and down. Paint in pastel colors. Purchase a 24" circular piece of heavy glass (make sure edges are smooth) for a table topper.

1 square = 2"

147

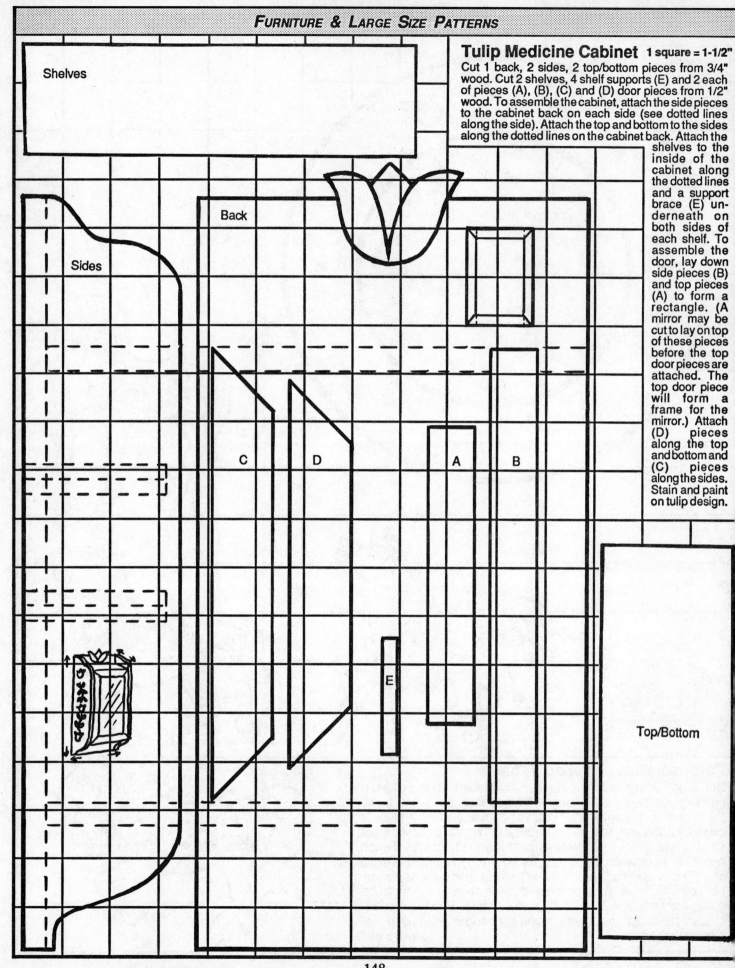

Shelves

Sides

Back

Tulip Medicine Cabinet 1 square = 1-1/2"

Cut 1 back, 2 sides, 2 top/bottom pieces from 3/4" wood. Cut 2 shelves, 4 shelf supports (E) and 2 each of pieces (A), (B), (C) and (D) door pieces from 1/2" wood. To assemble the cabinet, attach the side pieces to the cabinet back on each side (see dotted lines along the side). Attach the top and bottom to the sides along the dotted lines on the cabinet back. Attach the shelves to the inside of the cabinet along the dotted lines and a support brace (E) underneath on both sides of each shelf. To assemble the door, lay down side pieces (B) and top pieces (A) to form a rectangle. (A mirror may be cut to lay on top of these pieces before the top door pieces are attached. The top door piece will form a frame for the mirror.) Attach (D) pieces along the top and bottom and (C) pieces along the sides. Stain and paint on tulip design.

C

D

A

B

E

Top/Bottom

Rocking Horse

Cut 1 head, 2 head braces, 2 sides, 1 seat, 1 tail, 2 chest & rump braces and 6 underneath braces, all from 3/4" wood. Drill a hole through the head piece for a 1" dowel for a hand grip. Drill holes in the sides for a 3/4" dowel for a foot stirrup. (Foot stirrup dowel should extend through both side pieces. Make sure there is enough room for feet to rest on the dowels.) Assemble using the diagram as a guide. Stain or paint. Coat with polyurethane. Care should always be taken with toys for small children. Any rocking horse can tip over. Therefore, a child should be watched carefully when playing on this or any rocking horse.

1 square = 1-1/2"

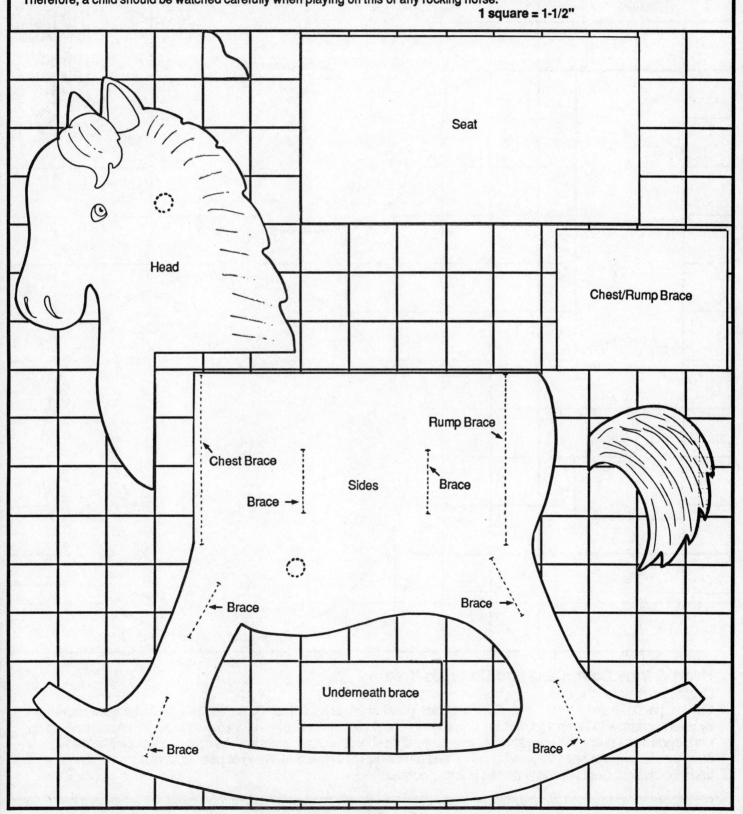

Seat

Head

Chest/Rump Brace

Rump Brace

Chest Brace

Sides

Brace

Brace

Brace

Brace

Brace

Brace

Brace

Underneath brace

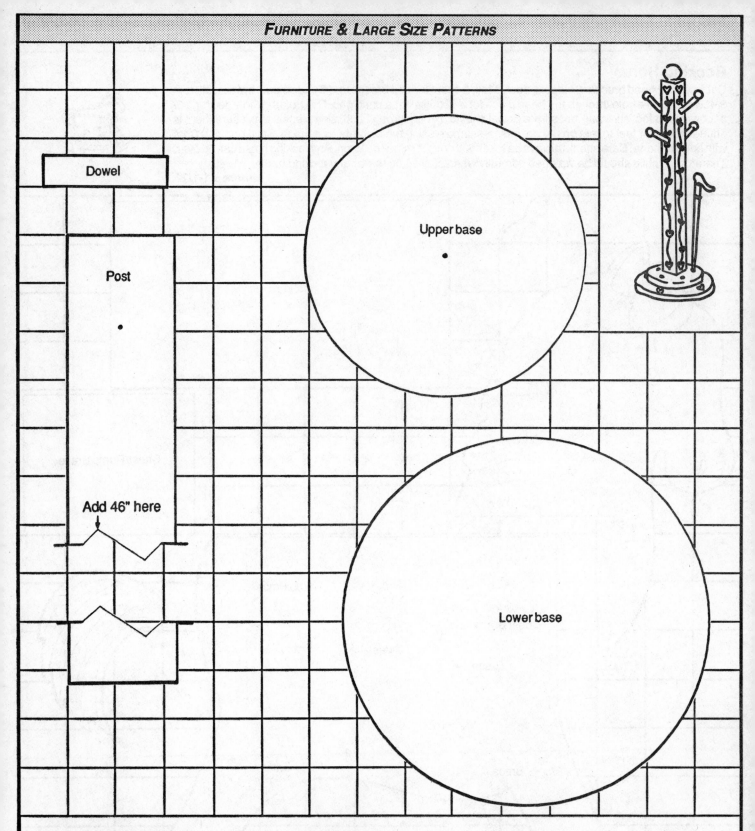

Dowel

Post

Upper base

Add 46" here

Lower base

Heart & Vine Coat, Cane and Umbrella Tree
Overall finished height: 60"

Cut 1 upper base and 1 lower base. Cut 1 coat rack post from 4 x 4 stock (add 30" as indicated). Drill holes as indicated by dots and arrow to insert 1" dowel. (1" dowel holes should be drilled 1" deep at a 45 degree angle.) Assemble, using the diagram as a guide. Wooden spheres may be purchased for the dowel ends and the coat rack top. Drill holes through base pieces to make rests for walking canes and umbrellas (see diagram). Stain or paint coat rack and paint on heart and vine design. Coat with clear acrylic finish or polyurethane.

1 square = 1-1/2"

Noah's Ark Child's Bedroom Set

This set includes a twin size headboard, a cabinet, a toy box and a matching peg rack. Instructions are included for each pattern. Furniture may be cut from large sheets of superior grade plywood. (Many people prefer pine or birch.) If using pine shelving, pieces may be glued together.

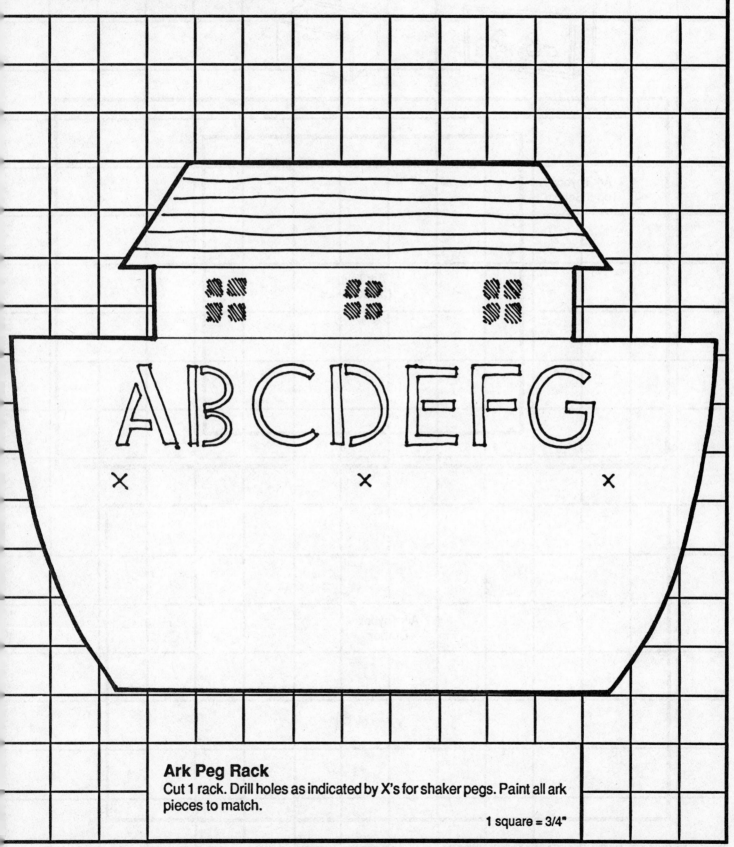

Ark Peg Rack

Cut 1 rack. Drill holes as indicated by X's for shaker pegs. Paint all ark pieces to match.

1 square = 3/4"

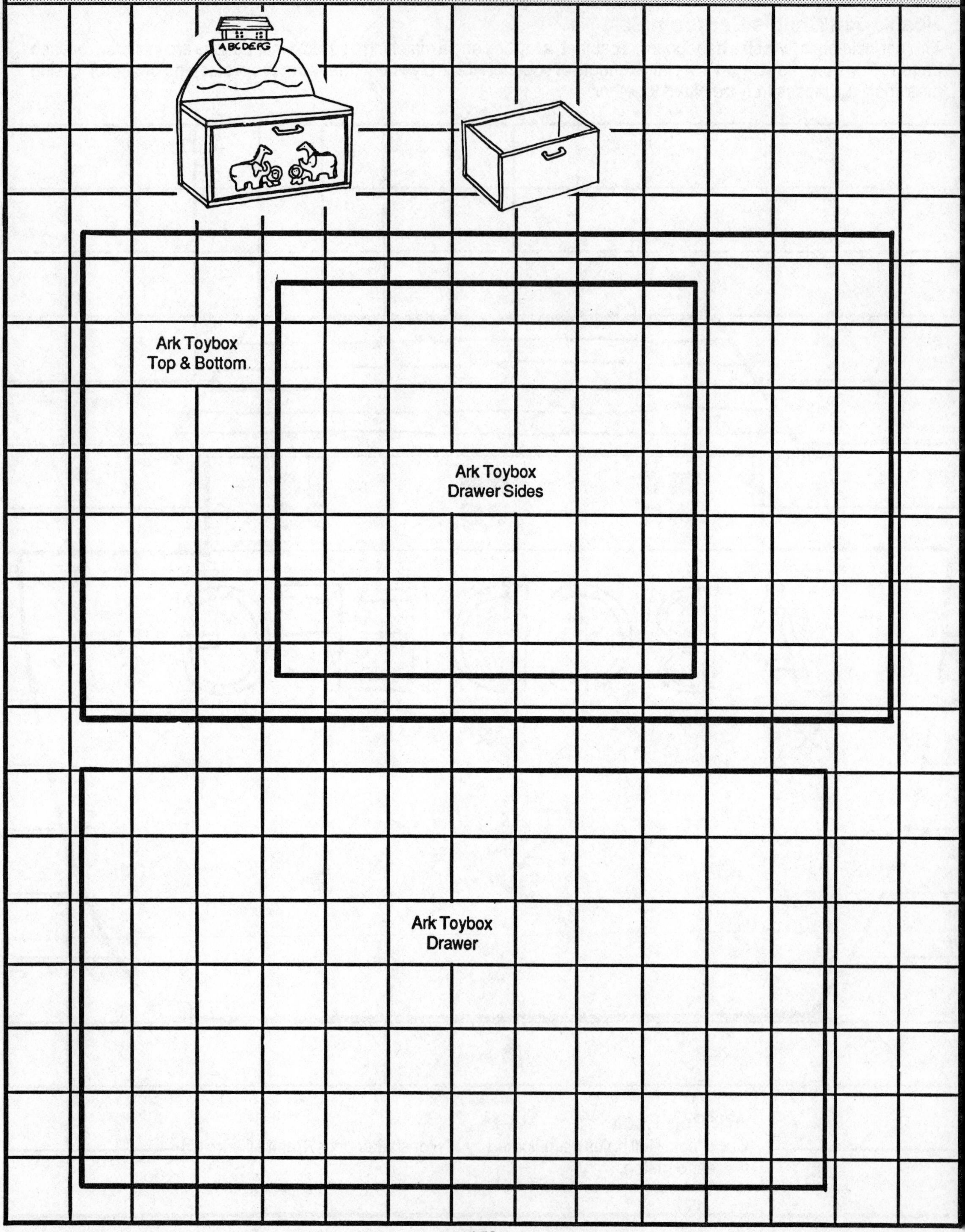

Ark Toybox
Top & Bottom

Ark Toybox
Drawer Sides

Ark Toybox
Drawer

Ark Toybox Seat

Overall finished size: 20" x 24".

For toybox: Cut 1 ark back, 2 top/bottom pieces, and 2 side pieces.

For toybox drawer: Cut 2 front/back pieces, 1 bottom piece and 2 side pieces.

Assemble the toybox according to the diagram. Assemble the drawer. Purchase a drawer pull to fasten to the drawer front. Optional: Use the animal patterns for the headboard and cut them from 1/4" wood. Finish and glue to the front of the drawer. Or, use the animal patterns to paint or stencil on the drawer front.

1 square = 1-1/2"

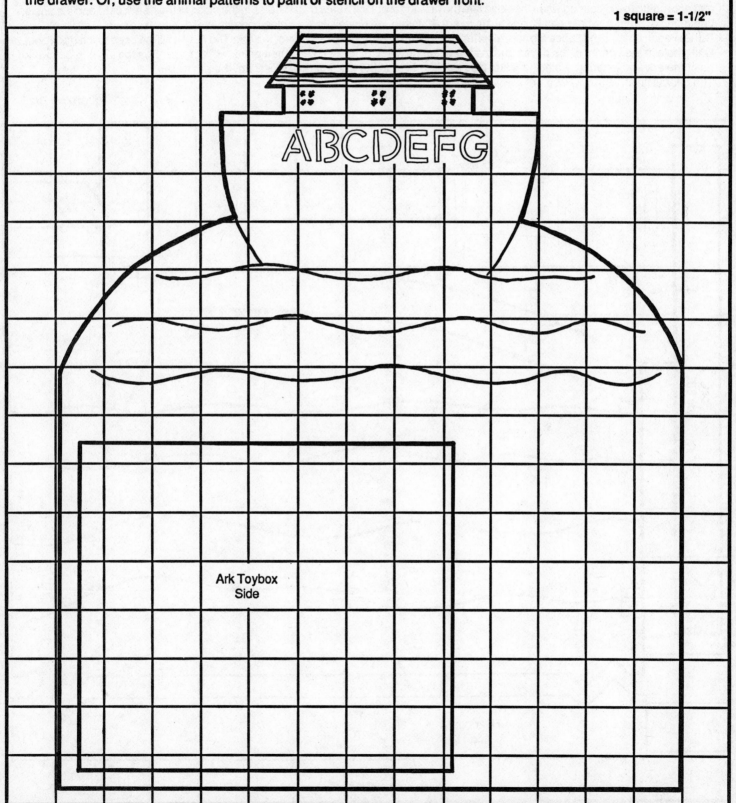

Ark Toybox
Side

Noah's Ark Twin Headboard

One half of the pattern is shown. Enlarge the pattern on a very large sheet of paper, fold the paper in half and trace through on the other side so that the entire pattern is on one large sheet. Another way to transfer the pattern onto wood is to enlarge the pattern as it is, trace the first half onto the wood and turn it over onto the other side. Then transfer the other half onto the wood. The whole pattern will then be transferred onto the wooden piece, one half at a time.

Cut 1 headboard from a superior grade plywood or join 1 x 12 pieces (add 15" to the pattern as shown). Cut 2 posts from 2 x 2 stock (adding 33" to the pattern, as shown). Cut ten 3/8" dowels 1-1/2" long to attach the side posts to the headboard. Score each dowel and apply glue to the scoring when inserting into the headboard. Drill 5 sets of 3/4" holes in the sides of the headboard and the posts, beginning at point A. After point B, drill holes every 6". Insert the dowels in the holes and use wood glue to secure.

Cut 2 of each animal and space the lion, elephant and giraffe evenly on either side of the ark. The doves will be used to top each post. Drill a hole in the bottom of the doves and the top of the post and glue. Stain and then paint with acrylics. See the ark peg pattern to paint the ark and lettering. Paint the water blue and the land at the top a dark beige. Paint the ark red.

The overall finished size will be 44" x 48".

1 square = 1-1/2"

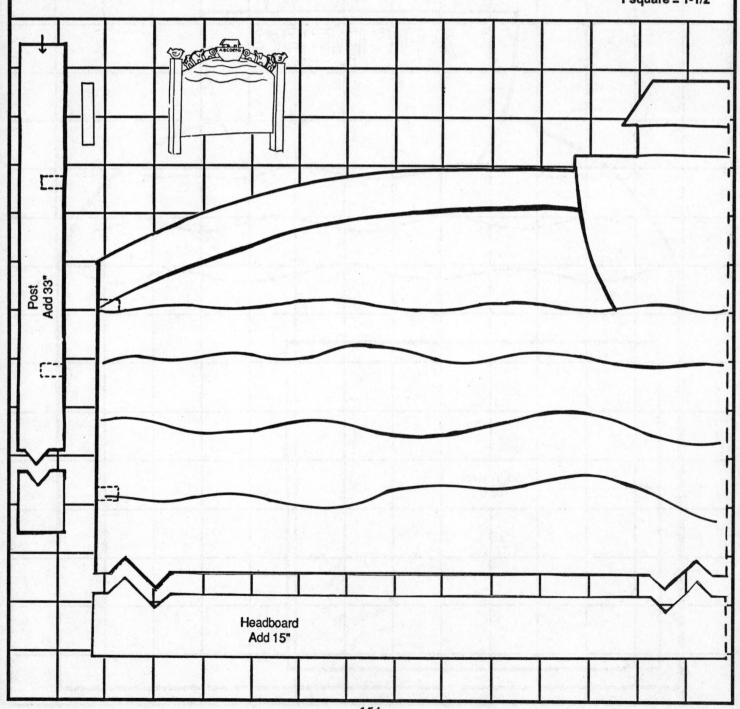

Post
Add 33"

Headboard
Add 15"

Ark Cabinet

Overall finished size: 28" x 22-3/4".

Cut 1 top, 1 back, 2 sides, 2 doors, 1 top shelf, 1 lower shelf from 3/4" wood. Assemble the sides and top to the back. The top shelf fits into the cabinet at the door bottoms. The bottom shelf should be attached (as shown) several inches from the bottom. Use finishing nails. Cover nail holes with wood putty and finish to match the Ark Set. Use the Ark Peg Rack pattern, trace it onto the doors and paint to match.

1 square = 1-1/2"

Ark Cabinet
Doors

Ark Cabinet
Top

Ark Cabinet
Shelves

Ark Cabinet
Sides

Ark Cabinet
Back

INDEX

159